Also Translated by Nancy T. Lin

IN QUEST:

POEMS OF CHOU EN-LAI

The cover picture, "The Soar," is contributed by the Chinese painter Cheng Shih-fa specially for this book.

REVERBERATIONS

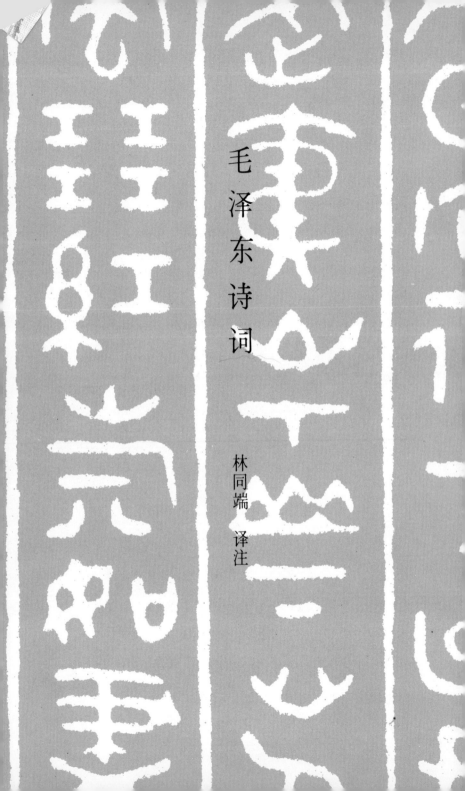

毛泽东 诗词

林同端 译注

REVERBERATIONS

A New Translation of
Complete Poems of Mao Tse-tung
with Notes by Nancy T. Lin

Joint Publishing Co., Hongkong

Published in Hongkong by
Joint Publishing Co.
9 Queen Victoria Street, Hongkong

First Published in 1980

Printed in Hongkong by
C & C Joint Printing Co., (H.K.) Ltd.
75 Pau Chung Street, Kowloon, Hongkong

Hardcover ISBN 962·04·0046·1
Paperback ISBN 962·04·0047·X

Publisher's Note

A couple of translations of Mao Tse-tung's poems have appeared in English. This new translation by Nancy T. Lin is the most complete English version so far published. It consists of forty-two poems of Mao's, including the three posthumous ones made public in September 1978. Of these three, two should be of particular interest to western readers: one sketching the poet's view on human history, and the other, a unique document, revealing the intimate personal side of his life.

The Notes have been carefully prepared and designed by the translator to give the necessary historical background and literary elucidations to the poems concerned. The reader will find them particularly pertinent and illuminating, showing as they do how each of the poems punctuates a landmark in the revolutionary career of the poet and in the stirring saga of New China.

Especially valuable is the incorporation in the Notes of the poet's own comments and explanations on points of dispute or miscomprehension among commentators and translators. Most of these authentic comments are available here in English for the first time.

The attached map indicating graphically places or scenes relevent to the contents of the poems will be visually helpful to readers.

"My guide (in translation)," says Nancy T. Lin, "has been to capture the best I can the central theme and ethos of each piece and transplant the essential images and dominant rhythm-waves involved." The quality she exhibits as translator of Chou En-lai's poems in her work *In Quest* is further demonstrated in this book, which the reader will enjoy reading for its veracity of execution and fineness of artistry.

Our thanks are due to the well-known painter Cheng Shih-fa for the cover picture he has specially conceived for the book. It helps bring out the rich import and beauty of the *Reverberations*.

Contents

Preface

Poetry as a rule defies adequate translation, the more so with languages so wide apart as Chinese and English in syntax, idioms and literary lore. In the following attempt with the late Chairman Mao's poems, my guide has been to capture the best I can the central theme and ethos of each piece and transplant the essential images and dominant rhythm-waves involved. While it is my hope to reproduce some measure of the original poetic impact, the result here presented may well be, I fear, just another sample of inadequate personal interpretation. Care has been taken to check up with authentic comments and group studies that have come to public attention to date. For errors that occur, the undersigned alone is responsible.

林同端

(Nancy T. Lin)

Huckleberry Hill
Lincoln, Massachussetts
U. S. A.

Note on the Notes

Notes to the poems are of two kinds: (1) Notes or comments given by the poet himself at various times. Some are not available so far in foreign translations; some marked "reported" are in all appearances authentic too, though not yet officially so acknowledged. They are of especial importance in view of a number of misinterpretations by commentators and translators. (2) Notes by the present translator, literary and historical, as deemed helpful for the understanding of the poems concerned. These are advisedly kept at a minimum, leaving more room, so it is hoped, for individual imaginative reading of the poems as such.

No attempt is made to go into the complexities of traditional Chinese prosody. Suffice it to say that Chinese poetry falls mainly into two divisions, *shih* and *tsu*. Of the *shih* forms, two are found in this collection: *seven-word regular (chi lu)*, which consists of 8 lines and 7 words to each line, and *seven-word short (chi chueh)*, which has 4 lines with 7 words to each — both subject to a more or less regularized scheme of tone and rhyme arrangements. The *tsu* genre comprises what were originally definite musical melodies in all varieties of length and form. Each *tsu* piece bears a special title which used to carry a specific theme for a specific occasion. But in time, the title is retained only as a key to the melody adopted, with no reference whatever to the theme or occasion involved. Latter-day poets are perfectly free, so to speak, to fill the old bottle with any kind of new wine they may individually prefer for the nonce. In this translation, the *tsu* titles are given simple English renderings in the notes, followed by the romanized equivalents, without further ado

3

about their respective historical origins or themes, which after all are not essential to the appreciation of the poems themselves.

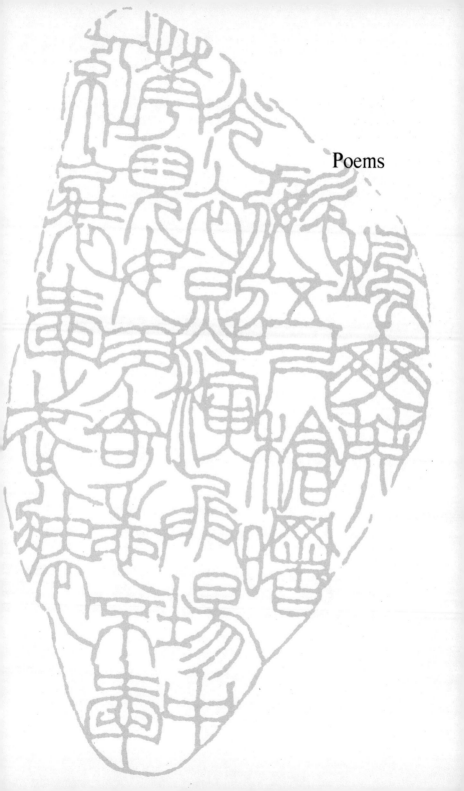

Poems

I

At Changsha

1925

Against the chill of autumn
I stand alone
At the tip of Mandarin Isle
Where the Hsiang bends north.
Look! the hills all crimson
With tiers of deep-dyed woods;
The river one translucent green,
And hundreds of barges busily plying.
Eagles cleave through the skies,
Fish glide over clear depths:
How on this frosty day Life strives for freedom!
Ah, boundless space,
Great earth in twilight's gray,
Who, I ask, is the lord of destinies?

I used to bring along
Companions a hundred strong.
Vivid yet those bygone days —
Rugged all and event-packed.
Schoolmates we were,
In the flower of strength and youth.
Impelled by resolve of intellect
We launched out full blast,
Fingers pointing at scenes unfolding,
Trenchant words lauding and decrying:
Potentates of the day — mere scum in our eyes!

And then, remember?
We breast-stroked in midstream —
How against the scudding boats
The waves splashed!

A *tsu,* to the melody *Spring in Chin Garden, Chinyuan Chun.*

Changsha: the municipal capital of Hunan Province, its first founding dating back to the Period of Warring States (475-221 B.C.). It has been known through the centuries for its political and strategic importance as well as for its literary lore connected with the ancient poet Chu Yuan and the Han essayist Chia Yi.

Mao Tse-tung's association with Changsha was particularly close. He came there in 1911 to stay for 8 consecutive years, a student in the provincial normal school and activist in anti-feudal and anti-warlord struggles. He founded the New Citizens Society, with a membership well up to 80 by the time of the May 4th Movement, 1919. After an interval of stay at Peking University (1918-19), he was back again to Changsha, editor of the *Hsiang River Critic.* He joined the Chinese Communist Party in 1921 as one of 12 original members, followed by years of intense activity in organizing labor strikes and peasant associations in Changsha and other parts of Hunan. This poem was written just before his departure from Changsha in October 1925 to take charge of the Training Center for Peasant Movement in Canton — a significant point in the revolutionary career of the poet.

The Hsiang River: largest river in Hunan, on which Changsha is situated.

Mandarin Isle: an islet in the Hsiang River just west of Changsha, so-called because of its famous mandarin oranges.

Various conjectures have been made as to the implications of the query on destinies in the last line of the first stanza. Presumably the poet has here in mind, more than anything else, the question of leadership of the proletariat or of the bourgeoisie — a crucial question much discussed then among the Chinese communists.

About the line *We breast-stroked in midstream,* the poet noted in December 1958: "This refers to swimming. I was a beginner then. In the flooding torrents of high summer, I was near-drowned on several occasions. A group of us persisted, staying dipped in the river even on severe winter days. "

II
Golden Crane Tower

Spring 1927

Nine streams course majestic through the Land;
One trunk-line, north to south, silently binds.
Misty drizzle spreads a haze of blue;
Tortoise and Snake guard over the Yangtse.

Gone is the Golden Crane — none knows whither,
Leaving this site to chance visitors.
A bowl of libation to the rushing surge below,
The tide in my heart mounts as the waves foam.

A *tsu,* to the melody *The Pusaman Amazons, Pusa Man.*

Written in Spring 1927 on the eve of the collapse of the Great
Revolution, the poem reveals a foreboding feeling and a silent resolve to
fight on. In summer, on August 7, the Emergency Session of the CPC
decided on armed struggle. With this, the Chinese Revolution entered
on a new stage — the build-up of rural revolts.

Golden Crane Tower: Situated on the Golden Crane Cliff west of
Wuchang, Hupei, the tower was first erected in the time of the Three
Kingdoms (220-280 A.D.) in commemoration of a Taoist immortal
who, as the legend has it, rode past the site on a golden crane's back. It
has since been a popular place of pilgrimage, made especially famous by
Tang poets, among them Tsui Hao and Li Po.

Nine streams: the various tributaries of the Yangtse River in Hupei and Kiangsi Provinces.

One trunk-line: the Peking-Hankow-Canton Railway, the sole line of railroad communication between north and south China before liberation.

Tortoise and Snake: two hills at Hanyang and Wuchang respectively, which directly face each other from opposite banks of the Yangtse. On them stand now the bridge heads of the Yangtse Bridge at Wuhan, completed in October 1957. Wuhan is the name for the well-known tri-city, consisting of Wuchang, Hankow and Hanyang.

III
Chingkang Mountain

Autumn 1928

Flags and banners stud the mountain side,
Drums and bugles rally on the top.
Let the enemy come
With their thousand-ringed siege.
Unmoved we stand —
A towering rock!

Guarded forts and vigilant watch;
A citadel, too, of united wills!
Then — the burst and boom
Of the reports of guns from Huangyangkai:
The enemy, oho,
Have scuttled at night!

A *tsu*, to the melody *Moon over the West River, Hsichiang Yueh.*

Chingkang Mountain: now known throughout the country as the cradle of revolution. Striding the border between Hunan and Kiangsi, the mountain covers an area of 250 kilometers round, with terrains of strong natural defense position. Here in September 1927 Mao established with some 1,000 men the first rural base of Red power, joined by forces under Chu Teh and Chen Yi in April 1928.

Huangyangkai: one of the five strategic passes that lead up to Chingkang Mountain. On August 30, 1928, Kuomintang troops launched four successive attacks on Huangyangkai and finally withdrew with heavy losses. In explaining the last lines of the present poem, Chen Yi, himself a poet, made it clear in a lecture on Mao's poems some time in May 1962 that the boom of guns here refers to the volleys of enemy fire designed to protect their rear on retreating.

The poem stands as an apt memento to the successful defense of the Chingkang base. A little over a month's time after the poem, Mao wrote his momentous article *Why Is It That Red Political Power Can Exist in China?*

IV
War between Chiang and Kwangsi Warlords

Autumn 1929

A sudden shift of Wind-and-Cloud:
The broils of warlords again!
Sorrows rain thick upon men
For another bubble of Millet-Dream.

Red flags, leaping the Ting River,
Fly straight over Lungyen and Shanghang.
Bits of the Gold Vase are back in our hands,
On with the redivisions of land!

A *tsu*, to the melody *Tranquilized Notes, Ching-ping Yueh.*

The war occurred in spring 1929 when quarrels among old and new warlords took a precipitous turn. Mao proposed to take advantage of the situation to extend Red power in the western parts of Fukien and Chekiang as well as in Kiangsi. He set out at once from Chingkang Mountain for Fukien and succeeded in October in consolidating new bases in west Fukien comprising Lungyen, Shanghang and other points, where the heavy concentration of land ownership in the hands of big landlords particularly called for an immediate land redistribution.

Wind-and-Cloud: a literary term meaning political constellation or situation.

Millet-Dream: a term derived from a Tang dynasty story where a Youth Lu dreamed, over a pillow given him by a Taoist priest, of a complete

14

fulfilment of all his worldly ambitions, only to wake up and find himself the same old non-entity lying in the same roadside inn, and the millet porridge he had begun cooking for himself was still cackling on the stove.

The Ting River: Issuing from Mount Kuanyin on the Fukien-Kiangsi border, the river passes Changting and Shanghang on its course to Kwangtung Province.

The Gold Vase: a classical metaphor standing for China's territory in unimpaired integrity.

V
Double-Nine Festival

October 1929

Age tells on man, but scarcely on nature:
Ever a Double Nine each year.
Here's the Double Nine again.
Chrysanthemums seen at the battle-front
Seem so much the lovelier!

Once more the autumn wind blows with rigor.
Unlike spring.
Better than spring! —
Silver frost, thousands of miles on;
A cerulean sky, one with the river!

A tsu, to the melody *The Mulberry-leaf Gatherer, Tsai Sang Tsu.*

Double-Nine Festival: so-called because it falls on the 9th day of the 9th moon, lunar calendar — popularly the day for scaling heights and flying kites. It has been associated for centuries with chrysanthemums (i.e. *huanghua,* yellow flowers) — a favorite theme for poets, who sing of "the lone fragrance in late autumn" and think of home and friends in "days of wind and rain." Mao comes up with this piece in a totally new spirit. Traditional motifs for a poem on the Double-Nine Day — chrysanthemum flowers, autumn wind, frosty sky etc. — have one and all acquired an ineffable aura of stout beauty and strength in the hand of a revolutionist who finds joy in struggle and sees unlimited prospects in trying circumstances.

About this poem and the preceding one *War between Chiang and Kwangsi Warlords,* together with poems VII, VIII, IX, X, the poet made the following observations on April 27, 1962:

"These 6 poems, hummed on horseback some time between 1929 and 1930, have altogether escaped my memory. Comrades on the editorial board of *People's Literature* have collected and sent them to me, requesting their publication. Herewith the slightly retouched version."

VI
New Year's Day

January 1930

Ninghua — Chingliu — Kweihua.
Dense woods, treacherous moss through a narrow path.
Whither our march today?
Straight to the Wuyi valley.
To the Wuyi valley we go,
With red flags flaunting in the wind —
A matchless tableau!

A *tsu,* to the melody *As If in a Dream, Ju-meng Ling.*

The famous Kutien Meeting in December 1929 laid down the proletarian military line with its double emphasis on Party's authority and links with the people, which eventually set the Red Army in a new mould, ideological and organizational. Action was at once taken to open up new bases in south Kiangsi. From Kutien, west Fukien, the Red forces struck north through Chingliu, Kweihua, Ninghua and then westward to Wuyi Mountain on the Fukien-Kiangsi border.

This poem, written en route, reflects the confident mood of the growing Red power, having now well over 60,000 regular troops over some 15 liberated areas. Four days later, on January 5, Mao published his famous article *A Single Spark Can Start a Prairie Fire.*

VII
On the Road to Kwangchang

February 1930

The skies blaze white.
We march through the snow,
The more set for the fight.

Overhead, the mountains mass.
Red flags, flapping in the wind,
Sweep across the Great Pass.

Where from here must we go?
Down the River Kan
In a maze of raging snow.

For the word yesterday says it straight:
A hundred thousand workers and peasants
Shall march upon Chi-an, to liberate!

A *tsu*, to the melody *Mulan Blossom (Shorter Version)*, *Chientsu Mulan Hua*.

After taking a number of counties in east Kiangsi in 1930, the Red Army climaxed the campaign with nine attacks on Chi-an, the principal city in central Kiangsi, between February and October. The liberation of most parts of southeast Kiangsi in the year paved the ground for the institution of the Central Red Area with Juichin as its headquarters.

19

This poem was written on the way to Kwangchang, an important county in east Kiangsi, pending the engagement at Chi-an further west.

Mountains mentioned in the poem refer most probably to the mountain ranges in the Yutu-Ningtu region north of Juichin.

The Kan River is the largest river in Kiangsi and Chi-an is situated just at its mid-course.

VIII
From Tingchow to Changsha

July 1930

We are the hosts of June's fire
Out to scorch the sinful and corrupt.
The Magic Cord of myriad yards in our hands,
The rocs and whales we'll surely truss.
Hail the battalions of Huang Kung-lueh:
That whole tract by the River Kan flames red!

A million workers and peasants
Combat-fit and eager to a man,
We sweep through Kiangsi,
We storm toward Hunan and Hupei.
We launch the stirring *Internationale*
As the whirlwinds join us from on high.

A *tsu,* to the melody *Butterfly Courts Flowers, Tieh Lien Hua.*

The adventurist line of Li Li-san calling for a general offensive against
urban centers resulted in reverses under the walls of Changsha and other
cities in summer 1930. Mao was then busy consolidating rural bases
back in Fukien when he was obliged to march to Changsha's rescue
from Tingchow, west Fukien. He succeeded, however, in dissuading the
Party from pursuing the mistaken strategy and directed his forces
actually to extending further the rural zones in west Kiangsi and east
Hunan. In extolling the deed of Huang Kung-lueh and the spread of

Red power, the poem has primarily these rural successes in view, achieved as they were in spite of the losses elsewhere under Li Li-san's leftist opportunism.

Huang Kung-lueh, a co-provincial of Mao's and a valiant commander in various revolutionary campaigns. He faithfully adhered to the rural-oriented policy of Mao's until he fell in action near Chi-an in October 1931.

The Magic Cord is derived from the remark of a Han dynasty scholar Chung Chun, who proposed to the Emperor of Han that he truss the King of Southern Yueh with his "long cord" on his volunteer mission there, and deliver the King to the imperial court — the term having been used since to mean an invincible weapon.

IX
Breaking through the First "Encirclement"

Spring 1931

Trees of tumultuous red singe the frosty sky
As wrath of the titans mounts to heaven.
Fog thickens over Lungkang,
Thousands of craggy cliffs soon darken.
All at once, the cheers arise:
Vile Chang Hui-tsan is captured alive!

Then, blasts of reeking smoke from mid-air:
Back to Kiangsi, a horde of two hundred thousand.
Roused and rallied,
Workers and peasants, tens of millions,
Unite in one cause, one mind.
O, the restless red flags below Puchou Mountain!

A *tsu,* to the melody *The Proud Fisherman, Yuchia Ao.*

Toward the end of 1930, Chiang Kai-shek launched his first "encircle-ment" campaign against the Central Red Area in Kiangsi with a force of 100,000 men. The decisive battle took place near Lungkang (a town about mid-way between Kwangchang and Chi-an) on the foggy morning of December 30, resulting in a rout of Chiang's troops and the capture of Chang Hui-tsan, their chief field commander. .

In spring 1931 Chiang sent his chief lieutenant Ho Ying-chin to

Nanchang with a force of 200,000 and began busily preparing for the second "encirclement." The present poem was written in summer, the first stanza dealing with the battle at Lungkang, the second with the preparations for the second contest.

Puchou Mountain is taken from the ancient legends about Kung-kung butting Puchou Mountain during his fight against the ruling dynasty of Chuanhsu. In using Puchou Mountain to symbolize the seat of Red power, the poet made a special observation as follows:

"Stories differ. I'm in favor of the version in Astronomical Notes, *Huainantsu*, which represents Kung-kung as the conquering hero. See what it says: 'In his wrath, Kung-kung butted Puchou Mountain, breaking the pillars of heaven and snapping the moorings of the earth. Thereupon, the sky tilted to the northwest and with it, the sun, the moon and the stars; the earth gaped in the southwest, where mire and water gathered.' Apparently Kung-kung didn't die, he triumphed."

Incidentally, it may be noted, Kung-kung in Chinese means concerted labor.

X
Breaking through the Second "Encirclement"

Summer 1931

Clouds rear above Paiyun Hill
As battle-cries intensify below.
Look! the stubs and stumps
Do stir and strive too!
Then forests of bayonets close in,
From beyond the skies
Winged hosts come swooping on the scene.

Seven hundred *li* in a fifteen-day drive:
Kan rivers with their hazy blue,
Ming hills in their jade green.
Facilely as mat-folding, the enemy hordes
Are by the thousand swept away clean.
Someone is weeping,
Vainly sighing over his "fort at every step"!

A *tsu,* to the same melody as in Poem IX.

Failing in his first attempt, Chiang was now adopting the strategy of "a fort at every step." After establishing a battle front of 800 *li* from Chi-an eastward to Chienning in west Fukien, he began his second "encirclement" operations in April 1931 under the slogan of cautious advance and gradual closing in. Mao countered with his famous alternating tactics of evasion and surprise attack and succeeded in luring the enemy to Paiyun Hill, southeast of Chi-an, where the main Red forces had concentrated in ambush. Engagement took place on May 16, when a surprise frontal attack brought about a break-through for the Red Army, followed by four successive quick battles to the north and then eastward to Kwangchang and Chienning – a 700 *li* drive in 15 days. From Chienning, Mao at once set about extending new bases over that part of the Kiangsi-Fukien border in anticipation of Chiang's next move.

Kan rivers in the poem refer to the various tributaries of the Kan River while *Ming hills* mean chiefly the Wuyi Mountain ranges around Chienning.

Someone weeping alludes ironically of course to Chiang Kai-shek's lament of failure which cost him 10,000 dead and 30,000 captured.

XI
Tapoti

Summer 1933

Red, orange, yellow, green, blue, indigo, violet.
Who's dancing in the skies with this colorful band?
After a shower, the sunset's glow:
The Pass and hills, with their verdured gushes!

A fierce battle raged here once.
Bullet-riddled — those village walls.
They've hollowed the site,
The fairer to look upon today!

A *tsu*, to the melody *The Pusaman Amazons, Pusa Man.*

Tapoti: a picturesque hill town some 50 *li* north of Juichin, the headquarters of the main Red base. Mao took several inspection trips to the vicinity in summer 1933 while Chiang Kai-shek, failing in his fourth "encirclement" campaign in March, was hectically preparing for the fifth. This poem was written during one of those inspection trips.

The poet, on passing Tapoti, dwelled with a painter's eye on the rainbow scene over the hill and recalled the fierce battle he fought on the spot against Chiang's pursuing troop back in February 1929 when he at the head of a Red contingent from west Fukien was engaged in opening up new rural bases in southeast Kiangsi. The last line, characteristically, niches his thought in the present with a swift turn.

XII
At huichang

Summer 1934

Near-dawn in the east.
Do not say it's too early
That we take the road.
We've trod every hill beautiful
And are young still.
Ah, the unique view
This side of the trail!

And those towering peaks
Beyond the Huichang walls.
How they rush in a tumble
Straight for the Eastern Sea!
But look, — our men point south —
There looms Kwangtung,
The more a mass of lush, lusty green!

A *tsu*, to the melody *Tranquilized Notes, Ching-ping Yueh.*

October 1933, Chiang Kai-shek launched his fifth "encirclement" attack with a force of a million men supported by 200 bombers. This, coupled with the mistaken policy of the Communist command which replaced Mao's guerrilla tactics with regular warfare, resulted in a loss for the Reds of practically all their bases in south China — the severest setback sustained after the debacle of 1927. It was in the critical days of July 1934 that Mao came to Huichang, the seat of the CPC's provincial branch for Kwangtung and Kiangsi. A meeting took place, where detailed preparations for what was to become the historic Long March were discussed.

The poem was written on July 23 when the poet, soon after breakfast, went up the Lanshan Peak outside the city for a lookout on the route of the journey. The comradely cheering tone of the piece is typical of Mao's in times of severe trials. "China is a big country," he said. "There is light in the west if night falls in the east; the north is open to us if the south darkens. There's always plenty of elbow room!" The Red Army was ready for the Long March.

XIII
Loushan Pass

February 1935

Keen is the west wind.
Across the vast sky
Wild geese honk to the moon of a frosty dawn.
A frosty dawn —
Horse hoofs clatter sharp,
Bugles sob low.

"Ironclad," they boast of this proud Pass.
But this day, in one stride,
We've left it well behind!
Well behind.
The hills are a sea of blue;
Blood-dyed, the sun dips!

A *tsu,* to the melody *Thinking of the Maid of Chin, Yi Chin-O.*

October 1934, the Long March formally began. After breaking through 4 blockade lines on its way from Kiangsi through Kwangtung, Hunan and Kwangsi, the Red Army reached Kweichow in December. In the deep of night, January 4, 1935, it entered Tsunyi, the second largest city of the province. Four days later a Party conference at Tsunyi definitely established Mao's leadership in the CPC. On January 19, the Red Army, a reduced force of 30,000 men now, struck north through the Loushan Pass, a strategic mountain stronghold leading to Szechuan Province, with a view to crossing the Yangtse at a point between Yipin and Luchow in Szechuan. Blocked by Chiang's troops, the Red Army turned back for the Pass, where it encountered Chiang's garrison on February 25 morning but succeeded in overcoming it in the afternoon through tactics of evasion and surprise attack. This poem was written right after the event.

The re-crossing of the Loushan Pass was a significant landmark in the saga of the Long March. For with it, the Red Army took a route further west over the Golden Sand River (the Chinsha River) at the Yunnan-Szechuan border which eventually led to Yenan, the destined goal.

Commentators have disputed over the time and scene of this poem. The following reported remark by the poet in February 1964 — authentic in all appearances — should settle the matter:

"Time: February. Frost in February, because it's warmer in the south. The incredulous will find this to be the case by a visit down south. The scene occurred on the same day, not on successive days. We left the Loushan Pass in the morning after encountering a strong enemy contingent, but took the Pass in the afternoon by a surprise comeback over a different route."

The first stanza, therefore, describes the morning scene and the swift covert march, while the second refers to the triumph in the afternoon, ending up with a broad scenic sketch of two laconic lines compelling in its suggestion of awe and destiny.

XIV – XVI
Three Poems to the Mountains

1934-1935

1

Mountains!
Whip and spur, I keep to the saddle all day.
I turn my head — lo!
The sky's but three foot three away!

2

Mountains!
As upset seas with giant billows swirling,
You splunge headlong —
Myriad steeds into battle hurling!

3

Mountains!
You thrust into the blue with unblunted tops.
The sky is falling —
You are the props!

Three *tsu* pieces, to the melody *The Sixteen-worder, Shih-liu-tsu Ling.*

Mountains, which constitute particularly the last sector of the Long
March, are here taken as symbols of the revolutionary might of the Red
Army and of the people at a time when the Japanese aggression was

penetrating within the Great Wall and the struggle against Chiang Kai-shek was reaching its final intensity. The first poem was apparently written in Kweichow, whereas the second and the third were written after the Red Army entered Szechuan. The three, however, form a unified whole, climaxing in the last two lines.

"The sky's but three foot three away" is taken from a folksong, which the poet notes as follows:

"Mount Skull above, Mount Treasure below:
The sky's but three foot three away.
Dismount if you come riding;
Head bent if you walk your way."

Mount Treasure (Papaoshan) is situated near Liping on the southeast border of Kweichow, which the Red Army passed in December 1934.

XVII
The Long March

October 1935

To men of the Red Army
Long marches are no daunts.
Tame are mountains and rivers
For all their parading thousands.

The sprawling Rocky Five
Seem but wavelets
That dance and frisk;
The massive sweeps of Wumeng
Skip lightly by —
Rolls of clay beads.

Now the Golden Sand
Laps the cloud-topped cliffs
With its warm wash;
Now the iron chains
Steal over the Grand Ferry
In an icy gleam.

Loveliest of all
Is the Minshan snow,
Glowing a thousand *li* across
As our three forces march smiling through.

A *shih* in seven-word regular, *Chi Lu.*

Starting from Kiangsi-Fukien bases in October 1934, the main body of the Red Army fought its way through Kwangtung, Hunan, Kwangsi, Kweichow, Szechuan, Yunnan, Sikang and Kansu and reached north Shensi in October 1935. There it was finally joined by the Second and Fourth Front Armies, resulting in the establishment of the new center of Red power at Yenan.

"Has history ever witnessed a long march such as ours?" said Mao in December 1935. "For 12 months we were under daily reconnaissance and bombing from the skies by scores of planes, while on land we were encircled and pursued, obstructed and intercepted by a force of several hundred thousand men, and encountered untold difficulties and dangers on the way; yet by using our two legs we swept across a distance of more than 25,000 *li* through the length and breadth of eleven provinces. Has history, we ask, ever known a long march to equal ours?" Commenting on the significance of the March, Mao continued: "It is a manifesto, a propaganda campaign, a seeding machine .... It has announced to some 200 million people in the eleven provinces that the road of the Red Army is their only road to liberation."

The Rocky Five (Wu Ling) refer to the chain of mountains running through the 4 provinces of Kiangsi, Hunan, Kwangtung and Kwangsi — so-called because of its five particularly well-known ranges.

Wumeng: one of the highest mountain ranges in the Yunnan-Kweichow plateau that overlooks the Golden Sand River on the north.

The Golden Sand (Chinsha River) is the name given to the sector of the upper Yangtse that flows through the western parts of Szechuan and Yunnan.

The Grand Ferry (Tatu River) is in west Szechuan with its famous bridge at Luting made of 13 iron chains with movable planks for floors spanning 300 feet across over rushing torrents. The Red Army succeeded by dint of audacity and deception tactics in crossing the Golden Sand in early May 1935 and effecting a spectacular forced passage over the Luting Bridge at the end of the same month.

Meantime, dissension had emerged within the CPC over the destination of the Long March. It was only at a Party conference at Maoerkai (in north Szechuan) in August 1935 that Mao's insistence on driving to Shensi definitely prevailed over Chang Kuo-tao's advocacy of retreating to Sikang. The decision had far-reaching ramifications. For the Japanese aggression had by then penetrated within the Great Wall, and only by establishing a base up north was the Red Army in a position to reach out to the rest of north China and then on to central China and the northeast and create an extensive network of resistance behind the Japanese lines — what eventually made possible the success both of the war of resistance and of the war of liberation.

From Maoerkai, the Red Army resumed their march north. By mid-September, it crossed Minshan, the massive range on the Szechuan-Kansu border with peaks of perpetual snow. "The Three Forces" mentioned in the concluding line refer to the main Red Army (i.e. the First Front Red Army which Mao was leading) and the Second and the Fourth Front Red Armies which had come across by different routes.

"With the crossing of Minshan," said the poet in 1958, "a bright unobstructed vista emerged. We had rounded the corner to the opposite phase, with verily 'shady willows and glowing flowers ushering forth a new village.' The few poems that follow reflect this mood."

This poem, written in the last days of September 1935, is said to have been read personally by the poet at a meeting of military cadres at Tungwei, Kansu, to the rousing cheers of the audience.

XVIII
Kunlun

October 1935

Rearing out of the earth,
A portent across the sky —
Wanton Kunlun,
You that have drained your cupful
Of this world's radiant spring,
You blow up wild
With your three million dragons of alabaster,
Plunging the universe in a convulsion of cold;
Then you let all melt and thaw in summer,
Flooding rivers pell-mell
So that men become fish and turtles.
Of your deeds or misdeeds these millenniums,
Who's been the appraiser and judge?

I should put in a word now, Kunlun:
You don't need that height,
Nor so much snow.
If only I could lean on the sky
And, sword drawn, split you in three —
One part as gift to Europe,
One part to the Americas,
One for the Eastern lands to keep —
That Great Peace might reign on earth,
A common heat and cold for the globe entire!

A *tsu,* to the melody *Fair Nien-nu, Nien-nu Chiao.*

Kunlun is the largest mountain range in China running across Tibet and Sinkiang. It reaches out to the Pamir Plateau on the west and extends into Chinghai, Kansu and Szechuan on the east. Its highest peak towers 7,719 meters above sea level. The Yellow River and the Yangtse have their sources in the southern sub-range of Kunlun, while Minshan is part of its central sub-range.

Kunlun has been sung in Chinese poetry since the days of Chu Yuan as the home of immortals and land of celestial bliss. Mao takes it in quite a different vein in this poem. "Anti-imperialism is the theme and no other," he said in a note in 1958 by way of clarifying the various conjectures over the implications of the poem. Kunlun here is apparently made to symbolize the colossal but irrational economic and social system of the past that must give way to a new order of universal equity and peace.

The poem is said to have been written while Mao was viewing Kunlun in the distance from the top of Minshan in a moment of respite that afforded him to utter his deepest thought and dream.

About *the dragons of alabaster,* the poet gave the following note:
> "A poet of old once conceived the snow scene as 'a battle among three million dragons of alabaster, filling the sky with torn nails and tattered scales.' I'm borrowing the image here to describe snow-covered mountains. For from the top of Minshan, one can see in the distance range after range sweeping away in a whirl of white even on summer days. These mountains, according to the folktale, used to be a mass of volcanic fire until Monkey King came along and put it out with the Banana-leaf Fan borrowed from a fairy. Since then, all have been white."

XIX
Mount Liupan

October 1935

The sky vaults high;
Clouds are light.
Wild geese flying south
Pass out of sight.
We've scored a march of twenty thousand *li*.
We shall the Great Wall reach,
Or no true soldiers be!

On top of Mount Liupan,
In the west wind's lap,
Red flags now freely
Flutter and flap.
The Long Cord in our hands at last —
When shall be the day
That we bind the Green Dragon fast?

A *tsu,* to the melody *Tranquilized Notes, Ching-ping Yueh.*

From Minshan, the Long March entered Kansu Province. Mount Liupan, running between Kansu and Ningsia with its principal peak towering 3,500 meters above sea level, is the last high mountain the Red Army had to cross before reaching its destination in north Shensi.

Surveying the landscape from the heights here in early October, the poet was taking a pause, as it were, to sum up the course of the journey so far and give a pointer on the next move.

The Great Wall: stands for the frontline of resistance against the Japanese invaders.

Green Dragon: alludes to Chiang Kai-shek, who, rather than Japan, so the poet said in a note in 1958, was engaging the immediate attention of the Red Army at the moment.

XX
𝔖now

February 1936

Landscape of the North —
Ice-bound a thousand miles round,
More miles on, wrapt in whirling snow!
Hushed from source to mouth,
The Grand River's pour;
Either side of the Great Wall,
One blinding vastness.
Mountains dance like silver serpents,
Tablelands rush on — herds of wax elephants,
One topping another in contest with the skies.
It takes but a fair morn
To touch this pure white with a blush of rose —
O, enchantment past compare!

Of such varied beauty is this Land and Realm,
Heroes unnumbered have vied in paying their court.
But ah, the Chin Emperor — the Han Monarch —
No giants of culture they were;
The Grand Sires of the Tangs and Sungs,
Scarcely adept in poetry;
And Genghis Khan,
Proudest at one time as Heaven's son,
Knew only bending the bow at the big eagle.
All are past and gone.
For manhood florid and full,
Look — the galaxy today!

A *tsu,* to the melody *Spring in Chin Garden, Chinyuan Chun.*

Written in February 1936, four months after the completion of the Long March and two months after the famous Wayaopao Conference of the Political Bureau of the CPC when the policy of a national united front of resistance against Japan was formally adopted and the creation of a "People's Republic" envisaged. "We Chinese," declared Mao, "have the spirit to fight the enemy to the last drop of our blood, the determination to recover our lost territory by our own effort, and the ability to stand on our own feet in the family of nations." The poem should be read against this background.

The Grand River refers to the Yellow River and *tablelands* to the highlands of Shensi and Shansi, north China. *The Chin Emperor:* the First Emperor of the Chin dynasty (259-210 B.C.); *the Han Monarch:* Emperor Wu of the Han dynasty (156-87 B.C.); *the Grand Sires of the Tangs and Sungs:* Emperor Tai-tsung of the Tang dynasty (599-649 A.D.) and Emperor Tai-tsu of the Sung dynasty (927-976 A.D.); *Genghis Khan,* the Mongol Emperor who reigned 1206-1227 A.D..

The lines about these outstanding rulers are meant to be criticisms rather than eulogies. This the poet made clear in the following note in 1958:
> "A protest against feudalism, a critique on one of the reactionary phases of the 2000-year feudal order. *Culture, poetry, the big eagle* — one can only give such touches here. For after all one is writing poetry. Would you call for violent invectives? Any other interpretation wouldn't be correct."

The concluding two lines, he said in the same note, "refer to the proletariat." In view of the various implications imputed to the above few lines, these notes by the poet himself should be of especial value.

The expression *feng-liu jen-wu* has several implications. I have made use of Walt Whitman's "manhood florid and full" as perhaps best suited to the context here.

42

XXI

Occupation of Nanking
by the People's Liberation Army

April 1949

As the host of our mighty million
Sweep across the Grand Yangtse,
A storm over Mount Chungshan
Spouts vapors of yellow and blue.
This citadel of the South
Does crouch tiger-like now
And coil with a dragon's majesty
Never known before.
O, the thorough overturn of Heaven and Earth!
The pathos and the joy!

So track down the desperate foe
In a last dash of valor;
Barter not, the Old Conqueror's fashion,
For an all-too-human name.
The sky would have wrinkled with age
Had it trifled with sentiments.
What marks the course of men
Is the Flood-tides and Mulberry-fields.

A *shih* in seven-word regular, *Chi Lu.*

With the order for a nation-wide offensive at dawn, April 21, 1949, the Red Army started the forced crossing of the Yangtse along a front of 500 kilometers between Kiukiang and Chiangyin and liberated Nanking on April 23 — what ended in effect the 22-year Kuomintang rule in China. The poem commemorates this historic event.

Chungshan, also called Hill of Purple Gold, is situated east of the city of Nanking. It has been described by classical writers as "a coiling dragon" while Nanking as "a crouching tiger" — both together constituting an imposing landscape suitable as a city for the nation's capital.

The Old Conqueror: Hsiang Yu, the warrior-tyrant of Chu in the third century B.C. who allowed his political rival Liu Pang to occupy the western part of the empire and gained a reputation for magnanimity, only to find his life and domain lost to Liu a couple of years afterwards. In his warning against repeating the mistaken policy of Hsiang Yu, the poet is alluding to the counsel of compromise with Chiang Kai-shek then current both within and without the CPC.

Flood-tides and Mulberry-fields, a traditional figurative phrase meaning the vicissitudes in this transient world, is based on the ancient story of Fairy Maku who had three times seen the surging sea dry up and turn into fields grown with mulberry trees. The metaphor is used by the poet here to suggest rather the law of change as the inexorable dialectics of nature and history.

XXII
Reply to Mr. Liu Ya-tsu

April 29, 1949

I remember well
The tea we had in Canton
And the exchange of verses in Chungking
When the leaves were yellowing.
That after thirty-one years
I should be back in this ancient capital,
Reading your exquisite lines
Against a sky of fallen petals!

Guard your heart
Against undue regret and sorrow.
Shouldn't the shape and shift of things
Always be taken with a broadness of view?
Do not say then — Lake Kunming is shallow.
For watching fish at play,
It may well be better
Than the hermit's Fuchun River.

A *shih* in seven-word regular, *Chi Lu.*

Liu Ya-tsu: A participant in the Revolution of 1911 and supporter of
Sun Yat-sen's policy of alliance with the communists in the twenties,
Liu became eventually a sympathizer of New Democracy and a personal

admirer of Mao's. He was invited to the People's Political Consultative Conference in Peking in March 1949 as one of the "democratic personalities." He wrote a number of poems in warm praise of Liberation — followed, however, by one entitled *Private Thoughts* in which he evinced dissatisfaction and spoke of desire to retire as a hermit to his home down south. Chairman Mao wrote the above poem in reply — a piece that by combining friendly regards with political exhortations embodies in effect the spirit of his well-known policy toward the intellectuals, the policy of uniting and remoulding them.

Tea in Canton: Back in 1925-1926 the poet had his first contacts with Liu while he was taking charge of the Training Center for Peasant Movement in Canton.

Exchange of verses in Chungking: August 1945, Mao came to Chungking for the parley on internal peace with Chiang Kai-shek. Liu wrote a poem in Mao's praise and Mao in turn showed Liu the poem *Snow* written in 1936.

Ancient Capital: i.e. Peking, which the poet first visited in September 1918 and to which he returned in March 1949.

Lake Kunming refers to the lake at the Summer Palace in Peking.

Watching fish at play: a pastime of literati and poets as part of their contemplative life.

Fuchun River: a river near Hangchow, where an East-Han dynasty hermit Yen Kwang preferred to live as a fisherman rather than accept Emperor Kwang-wu's offer of an official position. Mao here is mildly suggesting that Liu should stay on in Peking and take an active part in building new China.

XXIII
Reply to Mr. Liu Ya-tsu

October 1950

While watching performances during the National Day Celebrations in 1950, Mr. Liu Ya-tsu wrote an impromptu poem to the melody "Sands by the Washer's Brook." Herewith my reply, using the same rhymes.

Night hung heavy over the Crimson Land,
Day sought to break in vain.
A century of demons' reeling dance;
A ruined hearth for the five hundred million!

At the first cock, light dawns on earth;
From all quarters comes music of jubilance.
Our poet's spirits soar ever so high
At the rise of old Khotan strains!

A *tsu*, to the melody *Sands by the Washer's Brook, Wan Hsi Sha.*

October 1, 1949 Chairman Mao formally announced from Tien An Men the founding of the People's Republic of China and declared to the world: "The Chinese people have stood up and the days when China might be insulted and bullied are gone forever!"

October 1, 1950 saw the first anniversary of that auspicious date.

The present poem was written in reply to Liu Ya-tsu's impromptu verse composed on the 3rd evening of celebrations in the Hall of Cherished

Virtues (Huaijen Tang), where troupes of the minority peoples gave their performances as tokens of the grand unity of new China.

The Crimson Land is a classical nomenclature for China dating from the Warring States days.

A century of demons' dance alludes to the period of imperialist aggressions after the Opium War of 1840.

Five hundred million was the estimated population in China as known in 1950.

Khotan strains refer to a Kazak song *Full Moon* given by the troupe from Sinkiang which Liu specifically mentioned in his poem.

XXIV
At Peitaiho

Summer 1954

What a downpour on the Old North,
White breakers licking the skies!
No fishing boats off Emperor's Isle
Now remain in sight.
Over this expanse of flooding fury,
Where could they be?

Events traceable over a millennium ago:
Martial Tsao Tsao wielded his staff here.
"Eastward to Monument Rock" —
So testifies his ode to this day.
"The autumn wind whistles" as ever.
The world of men has changed!

A *tsu*, to the melody *Wave-washed Sands, Lang Tao Sha.*

Peitaiho: a well-known seaside resort on the Gulf of Pohai, close to Chinhuang Tao (Emperor's Isle), an ancient fishing port in east Hopei Province. Here in February 1954 the CPC held the fourth session of its Seventh Central Political Committee, and People's China had every reason to be proud of its achievements: the completion of the Land Reform that wiped out the basis of feudal economy and the proclamation of the General Line Program that set the nation forth to "building socialism." The year 1953 was one of especial significance:

the conclusion of the Korean War, the inauguration of the First Five-year Plan and the all-out drive for agricultural co-operatives throughout the country.

This poem was written in 1954 while the poet was summering at Peitaiho. No doubt he had in his mind's eye the changed look China was assuming. Characteristically, however, he starts with dashes of nature — the rain, the waves, the fishing boats and the fragmentary wanderings of an impressionist artist. With the second stanza, he roams leisurely into the remote realm of history and lights upon an episode pertinent to the locality — the emperor-warrior and his campaign and the legacy that was his ode. Apparently Mao's thoughts are a thousand years away. Yet deftly enough, he makes use of a bit of nature, of nature-in-history — "the autumn wind" in the said ode, and with a whirling turn plants us solidly in front of the present in four bold characters *huan liao jen-chien,* (the world of men has changed). China has changed, and with it the world! The astonishing potency — effortlessly achieved — of this laconic finale is one of the masterly strokes the poet has executed. And within a matter of a month or so, he opened the First People's Congress in Peking with the historic announcement:

> "We are prosecuting a most glorious and stupendous cause unprecedented in history. Our objectives shall be achieved and they can be achieved!"

Old North: means here Hopei Province, referred to in the poem as *Yuyen,* a classical name for the same region.

Tsao Tsao: Emperor Wu of the Wei Kingdom (155-220 A.D.) and statesman-poet. He led an expedition against the Wuhuan tartars in the north in 207 A.D. On passing Monument Rock (Chiehshih), a promontory south of Peitaiho but sunk into the sea since the fifth century, he wrote his famed ode *Visit to the East Sea* containing the lines "Eastward to Monument Rock" and "The autumn wind whistles" as quoted in Mao's poem.

XXV
Swimming

June 1956

I have just drunk the waters of Changsha
To come and taste now the Wuchang fish.
Swimming across the Grand Yangtse
With her thousand-mile surge,
I gain a full view of the broad Chu skies.
Let the wind blow and waves dash:
I sense Space today
As never in strolling any courtyard I can.
So said the Master by the river,
"How it flows ever on!"

Tortoise and Snake stand still;
Sails, wind-fed, shuttle in between.
Hence the birth of a Great Scheme:
A bridge shall fly across, north to south;
Nature's chasm shall be man's highway.
Walls of granite, too,
Shall rise on the west,
Turning back the Wushan Cloud-and-Rain
To conjure up placid lakes
On top of towering gorges.
Wouldn't the Fairy Maid,
Fair as ever perhaps,
Be startled to find her world
So utterly changed!

A *tsu,* to the melody *Water's Music: the Prelude, Shui-tiao Ko-tou.*

Socialist reconstruction came to a new high in 1956. The construction of the Yangtse River Bridge at Wuhan had begun and the conservancy projects for the Yellow River and the Yangtse were under way. Mao arrived in the Wuhan area in June on a nation-wide tour of inspection and wrote this poem after he swam across the Yangtse three times in four days — an event that led to the practice of yearly swimming meet throughout the nation since.

Waters of Changsha, according to the poet's own notes, refers to the famed White-Sand Well east of the city of Changsha.

Wuchang fish: Sun Hao of the Wu Kingdom (in the third century) contemplated moving its capital from Chienyeh (Nanking) to Wuchang to the opposition of the bureaucrats, landlords and the rest of the wealthier strata, who put up the slogan: Rather drink Chienyeh water than eat Wuchang fish. "Changes in sentiment have taken place," commented Mao humorously. "Wuchang fish is quite palatable in fact."

Chu skies: Chu is the classical name for Hupei and Hunan.

The Master: namely Confucius, whose well known remark is quoted here to convey the poet's own sense of the infinity of time and space, of movement and change.

Tortoise and Snake: see note under Poem II.

Nature's chasm: The Yangtse River has been so called in Chinese history, acting as it often did as the great divide between north and south China.

Walls of granite and placid lakes refer to the projects of the Big Dams over the Three Gorges on the Hupei-Szechuan border.

Wushan Cloud-and-Rain: Sung Yu's "Ode of Kaotang" (third century B.C.) tells of the Fairy Maid of Wushan Hill who assumes the form of a fleeting cloud in the morning and of swift rain in the evening; the phrase is used here to mean the torrents of the upper Yangtse.

The Fairy Maid is known in legends as the daughter of Red God, who died a valiant aid to the Great Yu in regulating the Big Flood and was buried on the southern slope of Wushan, where on top of Peak Feifeng (Flying Wind) a temple has been built in her honor. Once again the concluding line ushers forth the poet's favorite theme of change, theme of the triumph of man over nature.

XXVI
Reply to Li Shu-yi

May 11, 1957

I lost my proud Yang,
You your dear Liu. —
Light as *yangliu* in the wind, they soar
Straight to the Realm beyond the blue.
What, ah, has Wu Kang of the moon brought?
In outstretched hands he bears
A cup of *kwei* blossom brew.

Lone Chang-O steps out too,
Our martyr-souls to entertain.
Ample sleeves spreading, she whirls in dance
Ten thousand leagues over the skyey main.
There, comes word of Tiger Subdued on earth.
Tears of joy fly —
Lo, a downpour of celestial rain!

A *tsu*, to the melody *Butterfly Courts Flowers, Tieh Lien Hua.*

Li Shu-yi, a middle school teacher in Changsha, whose husband Liu Chih-hsun, an old friend of Mao's, joined the CPC in 1923, served as member on the Hunan Provincial Council and general secretary of the Provincial Peasant Association in 1926, and died in the Battle of Hunghu, Hupei in 1932. Li sent Chairman Mao in February 1957 a poem she wrote back in 1933 in her husband's memory. The above poem was

Mao's reply. It was originally entitled *Roaming Immortals,* a type of poetry made popular by Kuo Po (276-324 A.D.) with its descriptions of celestial scenes seen by the poets in dreams. "Different from the traditional pieces of this genre," Mao said in his letter to Li, "mine does not include the poet himself in the roaming, though samples of this are also found in latter-day *tsu,* as for instance those about the Double-Seven Eve."

The poem stands as a happy sample of the poet's imaginative skill of pressing classical myths into modern service, wherein the commingling of personal sentiment and revolutionist dignity reaches a rare height of dynamic balance.

Proud Yang   refers to Yang Kai-hui, Mao's first wife who joined the CPC in 1921 and died a 29-year-old martyr to the communist cause in 1930.

Dear Liu refers of course to Liu Chih-hsun.

Yangliu: literally aspen and willow, now indifferently used to mean willow or weeping willow. The term consists of the same two characters as the surnames Yang and Liu, forming therefore an apt pun that adds to the piquancy of the metaphor.

Wu Kang: a mythical figure condemned to the Sisyphean labor of cutting the huge *kwei* blossom tree (5,000 feet tall) in the moon, which healed itself after every stroke of his axe. Chang-O: another mythical figure who fled to the moon to live an eternal solitary life after secretly taking the elixir of life her husband Hou Yi the Archer had received from the Queen of the West. Wu Kang and Chang-O, as offenders of the powers that be, are apt rebel-images for the occasion of the poem. *Tiger Subdued* alludes to the ultimate overthrow of the Kuomintang rule in 1949.

[A word on translation is perhaps in place here for those interested. Insofar as poetry speaks through imagery, the translation of images requires especial care, the more so with Chinese poetry where the ideographic nature of the Chinese script often endows a word or phrase with a far greater power of visual suggestion and association than is possible in English. Take for instance the phrase *ching yang* (轻 飏) in line 2 of the Chinese original. Because of its *wind*-radical, the character *yang* carries a definite wind-image which is absent in its

English equivalent *soar*. To bring out the full image effect of the line, "Light as willows *in the wind* they soar" is actually a more adequate and faithful rendering than "Like willows they soar" as found in current translations. A subtler case exists with the verbal phrase *peng chu* (捧 出) in line 4. *Peng* means holding something with both hands; it carries in this particular context an implied *cup* or *flask*-image in addition to a *hand*-image. To translate it simply as "present" or "offer" is to strip off all the image richness of the original for a barren prosaic presentation. An express indication of the implied pictures of *hands* and *cup* is almost imperative. The same holds true with *wei jan* (巍 然) in Poem III and *sa shuang* (颯 爽) in Poem XXXI, where the *mountain*-image and the *wind*-image suggested by the radicals concerned are advisedly given their respective equivalents of *rock* and *breeze* in my translation.

— Tr.]

XXVII XXVIII
Good-bye, God of Plague

July 1, 1959

Thoughts and fancies come crowding to my mind after I read in the People's Daily, June 30, about the stamping-out of snail fever in Yuchiang County. I remain awake all night, when presently soft breeze brings along daylight warmth and the first gleams of the sun fall on the window. Scanning the faraway southern skies, I pen these lines in true gladness.

1

To what avail were our riches —
Green hills and waters blue?
The curse of a worm
And nothing could our Hua To do!
Villages sank in reed and rush;
Life drained away fast.
House after house desolated,
Ghosts sang triumphant.

Sitting here,
I speed with the earth
Eighty thousand *li* a day;
Circling the skies, I survey
The endless galaxies of Milky Ways.
There Star Cowherd — he is still anxious
For word on the God of Plague,
When lo! man's woe and fury's mirth
Are both set to flight
With the on-flow of time!

2

Myriad willows dance in the breeze of spring.
Land of Celestials —
Six hundred million strong
And each a sage, a titan!
At whose bidding —
Rains of rosy petals
Swell into a joy-surge;
Hills of primal green
Turn bridges of fond dream.
The firmament merges with the Rocky Five
At the fall of our silvery hoes;
The earth rocks with the Three Rivers
As our arms of steel strike.

Whither your retreat, O Lord Pestilence?
Our holy candles and paper boats
Shall light your way blazing to the skies.

Two *shih* pieces in seven-word regular, *Chi Lu*.

Snail fever or schistosomiasis was a wide-spread endemic disease in
pre-liberation China that affected some 350 counties in 12 southern
provinces, involving more than 10 million direct victims and upward of
100 million indirectly afflicted. For instance, in Lantienpang, a district
of 50 square *li* in Yuchiang County, northeast Kiangsi, more than 3,000
died of the disease in 50 years, leaving behind straggling survivors of
swollen bellies and shrunken limbs over 20 desolated villages and
14,000 *mou* of wasted farmland. The call for an extermination
campaign came in 1955. Yuchiang was the first county to achieve the
objective.

Hua To: a famous surgeon and doctor in the Period of Three Kingdoms. In a talk with medical workers March 12, 1966, Mao said:

"Medical workers in the past refused to contact the masses and showed little faith in them. But haven't ways of stamping out the snails been invented now by the masses? Hence the remark in my poem: The curse of a worm and nothing could our Hua To do."

Eighty thousand li a day: Differences in interpretation occurred. The poet made the following observations in a letter to Chou Shih-chao, November 25, 1958:

"There is ground for the figure given. The diameter of the earth is about 12,000 kilometers. Multiplied by the 3.1416 of the *pi,* it comes out roughly 40,000 kilometers, i.e. 80,000 Chinese *li* — the distance made by the earth's rotation (namely, distance made in a day's time)."

Star Cowherd: Niulang, a legendary youth who went up to heaven to become Star Cowherd on the Milky Way (known in astrology as the constellation of the Bear) and who is supposed to have a reunion with Star Weaving Maid on the opposite bank on the Double-Seven Eve (7th day of the 7th moon) every year. "China has created innumerable deities in the past 3,000 years," Mao is quoted as saying. "The Cowherd and the Weaving Maid alone are of the working people, two superb images of the working people belonging to an entirely different category from that of the God of Plague."

A sage, a titan: The original wording in the poem is *Yao and Shun,* two ancient rulers known for their sagacity and might. As the phrase is used here in figurative sense, a free rendering in English is advisedly given.

Rains of rosy petals: a literary expression for spring time rains which carry fallen flowers with them. This line together with the 3 lines that follow alludes to floods that are being turned into water power and inaccessible regions into developed areas.

Rocky Five: see note under Poem XVII.

The Three Rivers literally refer to the Yellow River, the Yangtse and the Pearl River, used here to represent rivers in China in general. *Holy candles and paper boats* are burned on occasions of popular exorcisms against evil spirits. Holy candles for *ming-chu,* i.e. candles used for sacrificial purposes — a term dating back to the ancient classic *Rites of Chou;* it has been wrongly understood as "candles lit" etc. by commentators and translators.

XXIX
At Shaoshan

June 1959

Arrived at Shaoshan June 25, 1959 after an absence of thirty-two years.

In dim dreams away from home
Still do I curse that long-fled past —
Thirty-two years ago
On this native soil!
Red flags flying,
The serfs rose —
Sticks pitted against whips
Which the scoundrel lords were wielding
High and mighty with hands infernal-black.
Many, many were those
Who laid down their lives in noble resolve,
Who dared to move Sun and Moon
To lay out a New Sky!

Happy now — I watch
This sea of paddy and corn
Surge in boundless green
As heroes from the fields around
Start homeward at the rise of evening smoke.

A *shih* in seven-word regular, *Chi Lu.*

Shaoshan: Mao's birthplace, a village 100 kilometers southwest of Changsha, surrounded by hills green with pines and cedars. Mao attended his primary school here before he left for the middle school in Hsianghsiang at the age of 16. He returned in 1924 to organize some 20 peasant associations, and again early in 1927 when he was making investigations of the peasant movement in Hunan with the consequent historic report in support of peasant uprisings.

This poem written a decade after liberation is not one of reminiscence alone, but an affirmation of the program for the People's Commune, as the concluding lines indicate, against criticisms within the Party and hostile assails from abroad.

In sending this poem and the next (Poem XXX) to the *Poetry Magazine,* September 1, the poet has this to say in comment:

> "It would be unthinkable if the great cause of 650 million people should have gone untouched by the wild furies and curses of the imperialists and their running dogs in various lands. The more violent their curses the better I feel .... These two poems are my answers."

Note a variant interpretation of line 4 in the Chinese original: "Black hands" is taken by some commentators to mean the powerful dirt-covered hands of the revolting peasants, who had succeeded in seizing the control once exercised by the landlords. (See *Selected Works of Mao Tse-tung,* Vol. I, "Report on Investigations of the Peasant Movement in Hunan," Section 6.)

XXX
Ascending Lushan

July 1, 1959

A single range
Soars up like a giant guard
By the Grand Yangtse.
Four hundred curves and turns
Spiral to a leap
On to its pinnacle of massive green.
Cool-eyed, I face the ocean
And survey the world below
As warm winds cleanse the river-borne skies
With laps of rain.
Clouds scudding across the Nine Streams
Set the Golden Crane afloat;
Torrents rush down the expanse of Triple Wu —
Bursts of foaming white!

Where, I wonder,
Might Magistrate Tao have gone?
Farming in the Retreat of Peach Blossoms —
Was that ever feasible?

A *shih* in seven-word regular, *Chi Lu*.

Lushan, one of the best known scenic hills of China, has been a favorite resort for literati and statesmen and an object of poems and songs through the centuries. Situated 20 kilometers south of Kiukiang, Kiangsi, it towers over the Yangtse on the north and Lake Poyang on the south, its highest peak rising 1,543 meters above sea level. Kuling, the resort center, is now accessible by bus over a road of 35 kilometers with some 400 turns and bends.

From Lushan heights, the poet's vision, ranging over the immense expanse of the Yangtse Valley, sees in the clouds and torrents veritable scenes of stirring socialist reconstruction (cf. the poet's note on *billows of Tungting Lake* under Poem XXXII). The concluding lines are meant presumably to refute utopian dreams that shun realities.

Nine streams and the Golden Crane (see notes under Poem II) represent the mid-Yangtse provinces with the industrial Wuhan area as the center.

Triple Wu, historically comprising Soochow, Changchow and Huchow, stands here for the rich regions of the Yangtse Delta.

Magistrate Tao: Tao Yuan-ming (356-427 A.D.), probably the most celebrated poet between the Han and the Tang dynasties, retired a hermit to the foot of Lushan after quitting his job as magistrate in Pengtse out of distaste for the need of "bowing to a higher official." He wrote the famous utopian essay *Peach Blossom Brook,* where a fisherman discovered an unknown colony in a valley upstream enjoying an idyllic life of simplicity and freedom away from the social and political turmoils of the outside world.

In connection with the line "Cool-eyed, I ... survey the world below," it may be pertinent to note that a couple of weeks before the poem's date Soviet Russia had unilaterally cancelled the 1957 agreement of supplying China with atom bomb secrets, and that the Camp David meeting between Khrushchev and Eisenhower was to take place in September.

XXXI
Militia Women : Inscription on a Photograph

February 1961

Fresh as breeze,
They march on with five-foot rifles,
Fair and brave in the first glitter of the sun
That wakes the parade ground.
China's daughters
Aspire high these days:
They take to the uniform
Rather than robe and gown.

A *shih* in seven-word short, *Chi Chueh.*

"In the masses of the people resides the most deep-seated source of fighting power." Such was Mao's basic thought, which gave birth to his grand strategy in the war of resistance against Japan and which led him to declare in 1938 that militia is the basis of victory. In 1958 he called for a nation-wide institution of militia. "Besides having a regular army, we must go in for militia forces in a big way, so that the imperialists in invading this nation shall be rendered incapable of budging an inch!"

The present poem *Militia Women* should be read in conjunction with Chairman Mao's theory of people's War, which had gained an added practical urgency by early 1961. For on top of intensified U.S. attempts at oceanic encirclement of China, Soviet Russia had followed up its unilateral cancellation of contracts and withdrawal of expert aids with a full dressed attack on the CPC at the Moscow Conference in

November 1960. Women, "half the heaven" as Mao elsewhere called them, are destined to play their due role.

XXXII
Reply to a Friend

1961

Silver clouds flutter over the Nine Mounts
As the Princesses stride the wind
Down the airy blue.
That twig of bamboo
Still speckled with their thousand tearstains,
And the myriad blossoms of roseate glow
Now over the rippling folds of their gowns!

Billows of Tungting Lake
Surge in whirls of snow against the horizon.
Songs the Long Islanders sing —
How they set the earth reverberating!
I'd often dream then of the cosmic vast,
Where the land of *fuyun* glory
Shall ever bathe in morning sunshine.

A *shih* in seven-word regular, *Chi Lu.*

Commentators have disputed over several points in the poem. The poet
has given the following elucidations:
    "A friend refers to an old schoolmate in Changsha. *Billows of
    Tungting Lake* alludes to the Big Leap Forward in Hunan
    Province. *Long Island* means Changsha, which was evolved from a
    sandy delta. Many people have lived in Changsha without

knowing the history of the locality. *Dream of the cosmic vast,* modeling after Li Po's line of 'dream of Wuyueh', represents just roving fancies of the moment. *Land of fuyun glory* comes from a line by Tan Yung-chih, a Tang dynasty poet: 'Myriad miles of autumn wind over the land of *fuyun';* it refers to Hunan Province. *Fuyun* here is hibiscus mutabilis, not lotus which blossoms in summer." (Reported comment, Feb. 4, 1964)

The Nine Mounts and the Princesses: The Mounts are in south Hunan, also called Hills of Tsangwu, where the legendary Emperor Shun is said to have died while taking his inspection tour in the region. His two consorts O-huang and Nu-ying (both daughters of the defunct Emperor Yao, hence traditionally referred to as the Princesses) hurried to the bank of the Hsiang River to lament over the death of their lord, so much so that the near-by bamboo trees were permanently stained with their copious tears and grew to be the spotted bamboo as known today.

The poem, starting with an imagined visit of the Princesses and ending up with a dream of a universe of sunshine, is another sample of the poet's characteristic of talking politics in terms of symbolisms of myth and nature.

It may be of added interest to note the recent reported remark of Mao's that while writing the first stanza, he was thinking of Yang Kai-hui, his martyr-wife, and "roseate glow," alluding actually to Morning Glow (Hsia-ku), was Yang's pet name. (See "Report of Interview with Lu Ti," *New Evening Post, Hongkong,* January 12, 1979.)

XXXIII
Fairy Cave, Lushan: Inscription on a Photograph

September 9, 1961

That pine tree —
Hale and sturdy against the twilight's gray:
How unruffled she is
In face of the riotous clouds
That sail tearing by!
And the unique Fairy Cave,
All nature-hewed,
Stands on the perilous summit
Commanding a boundless view!

A *shih* in seven-word short, *Chi Chueh*.

Written at a time when China was going through the critical years of natural calamities and international encirclement. The 22nd Congress of the Soviet Communist Party was to come in a month and a showdown on the ideological dispute looked inevitable.

The *pine* and *cave* images as presented in the poem are presumably meant for true proletarian revolutionaries who are capable of facing storms in equinimity and ready to run supreme risks in pursuit of communist ideals. "The pine," comments Mao, "standing erect and firm against the severities of winter, is a tree of high principle."

Fairy Cave: the famous natural cave at the Cliff of Buddha's Hand on the west side of Kuling, where Chou Tien, a Taoist immortal, is said to have dwelled once.

XXXIV
Reply to Comrade Kuo Mo-jo

November 17, 1961

No sooner had thunderstorm struck the earth
Than Demon rose from the heap of Pale Bones.
The Monk, foolishly erring,
Might yet be reclaimed.
But that goblin, that Evil Spirit,
Was a sure calamity to man.
Then Sun the Golden Monkey
Blazed forth with his mammoth club,
He purged this precious planet,
O, myriad miles round,
Of filth and dirt!

Viperous miasma is back again today:
To Great Saint Sun, our hearty acclaim!

A *shih* in seven-word regular, *Chi Lu*.

Kuo Mo-jo, the well known writer and head of the Chinese Academy of Sciences, saw a dramatic presentation of the episode in Peking in October 1961 and sent Chairman Mao a poem in which the Monk was denounced as a confounder of right and wrong deserving "a thousand sword cuts." Chairman Mao's reply is meant to rectify this view, with a definite topical implication characteristic of his practice. November 17, 1961, the date of this poem, falls exactly one month after the 22nd

Congress of the Soviet Communist Party under Khrushchev, and there is little doubt as to what the poet has in mind. *Thunderstorm* and *Demon* allude presumably to the dialectic relationship of Revolution and Counter-revolution. The main contradiction and struggle as has emerged is rather one between Demon the real enemy and Monkey the hero protagonist, while the Monk represents only the unawakened masses who are deceived and can be and should be educated and won over instead of condemned and alienated. Kuo's error is therefore no mean error of strategy for a revolutionist. The concluding line of the present poem is a clarion call to fight the forces of reaction in general and revisionism in particular.

Demon of the Pale Bones: Journey to the West, a Yuan dynasty novel, deals with the pilgrimage of Monk Tripitaka to India in quest of Buddhist sutras. With him as the chief fellow pilgrim and fighting guard was the Golden Monkey, the "Great Saint Sun" that had once sought to storm the heaven. Of the numerous evil forces the Monk encountered on the way, the Demon of Pale Bones was probably the wiliest, who succeeded in hoaxing the Monk into confidence and compassion despite Monkey's repeated warnings, but who was eventually subdued by the latter in three successive contests of magic power.

XXXV
The Winter Plum

December 1961

After Lü Yu's "Ode to the Winter Plum," *with a reversal in the theme.*

She saw Spring off in wind and rain.
She greets it back now, in sleet and snow.
Where icicles dangle a thousand feet down the cliff,
There she is, branch and blossom,
Pert in her splendor.

All splendor, she lays no claim to Spring,
She would only be Spring's harbinger.
When hills are glowing with flowers of all hues,
She stays in their midst,
Smiling ever.

A *tsu,* to the melody *The Fortune Teller, Pu Suan Tsu*.

The 22nd Congress of the Soviet Communist Party in October 1961 spelled out in effect the irrevocable finality of the Sino-Russian ideological break. This poem is the poet's answer. In short, China will not be cowed. China defiant shall be China triumphant. Not the triumph of a claim, but the triumph of a message, the aim and fruit of which is Spring destined for all, with China as an unobtrusive rejoicing participant.

The winter plum, for centuries the symbol of a forlorn scholar in self-appreciative purity, is here transformed into a personification of an inspired nation dedicated to a fighting ideal, or in the poet's eye in this case, of a true Marxist-Leninist Party at this specific juncture of history.

Lu Yu, a great Sung poet (1125-1210 A.D.) sang of the winter plum on some 100 occasions out of the 10,000 poems he wrote. The following is the specific piece Mao refers to in his note as shown above:

Beyond the post house, by a broken bridge,
She blooms to herself — all forlorn:
Sorrowful enough in the gray of dusk,
And by wind and rain further torn.

Let sister flowers their envies pour.
Parading in spring she'd disdain.
Blown and fallen she's ground into dust.
Her fragrance alone shall remain!

XXXVI
Winter Clouds

December 26, 1962

Snow —
Pressing through the winter clouds —
Breaks into swirls of hoary catkins.
Buds and blossoms
Have one and all shrivelled and fallen.
Blast after blast of icy waves
Pour furiously from the skies.
But out of Mother Earth,
The vital breath
Begins softly stirring!

True warriors will hunt down tigers and leopards:
Never shall the brave quail before a bear.
A world of whirling snow
Is the winter plum's joy.
Flies die frozen, so it should be!

A *shih* in seven-word regular, *Chi Lu.*

1962 was a year of precipitated developments. Khrushchev's proposal for a world-wide joint rule with the U.S. brought about the Anti-proliferation Agreement in August. His vilify-China campaigns culminated in the concerted attacks from the platforms of the conferences of five European Communist Parties in November. China took up the gauntlet.

On December 15, Peking published its first formal political-theoretical tract in denunciation of modern revisionism and followed it up with a powerful barrage of six others in three months. The first round of the Great Polemic had begun.

Written in the opening weeks of the Polemic, the present poem and the next (Poem XXXVII) have primarily this situation in view. The indifferent mixing of vernacular parlance and classical allusions is peculiarly effective in delivering the satiric punch desired.

XXXVII
Reply to Comrade Kuo Mo-jo

January 9, 1963

Just a couple of flies
Up against the wall on a dot of a globe!
They buzz, they hum,
Now in shrill complaint,
Now in broken sobs.
Gnats that talk glibly of uprooting an oak,
Ants vaunting of their Superpower on the Locust Tree!
The west wind is scattering sere leaves
Over the ramparts of Chang-an —
Let fly the Ringing Arrow!

So much to do,
Always in urgency!
Heaven and earth revolve,
Night and day press on.
Millenniums are far away.
The moment is all!
The four seas are heaving in swells of tidal fury,
The five continents rocking with thunderstorms.
Away with all pests to men!
The cause is irresistible.

A *tsu* to the melody *A River All Red, Man Chiang Hung.*

Kuo's poem speaks of the world-historic significance of Chairman Mao's leadership and his thought. Mao, however, is availing himself of the occasion to take stock of the world situation as it then exists. The ideological dispute with Soviet Russia is evidently uppermost in his mind. The topical references of flies, ants and gnats are unmistakable, alluding as they do respectively to the vilifying campaigns, the big-nation chauvinism and obstructionist tactics of the Soviets.

Whereas Poem XXXVI speaks of blasts of icy waves, the present poem points to the tidal swells and thunderstorms, i.e. the world-wide movements for independence and liberation among the oppressed nations and oppressed people — what has of late years crystallized into the fighting concept of "the Third World" of which China has declared herself a part. The confidence expressed in the finale reiterates a basic tenet of the poet's — the people of the world are destined to win.

Ants and the Locust Tree: A Tang dynasty story by Li Kung-tso tells of a certain Chunyu Fen dozing under a locust tree and dreaming of becoming an eminent prefect in the Great Locust Kingdom, which he found on waking up to be just an ant-hole under the tree, soon to be washed out too by a storm in the same night. *Gnats and the oak* is derived from lines by Han Yu, a Tang poet:

> Gnats trying to topple a giant tree,
> Ludicrously ignorant of their own impotence.

The west wind scattering sere leaves over Chang-an: a recast from lines by another Tang poet Chia Tao, alluding here to the essentially decadent state of reactionaries. *Ringing Arrow:* arrow with a special whistle attached, shot in ancient days as a signal for battle; it alludes here, among other things, probably to the launching of the Great Polemic in particular.

XXXVIII
Chingkang Mountain Re-ascended

May 1965

I have long wished
To soar above the clouds,
Re-ascending Chingkang Mountain.
Here I am,
From a thousand miles away,
Back among haunts of old:
Now transformed — a visage all new!
Everywhere —
Orioles carol, swallows dip,
Springs gush and gurgle,
Steep roads thrust to the skies.
Huangyangkai crossed:
No terrains, however forbidding,
Could challenge our sight.

Thundering storms,
Battling standards:
Humanity on the march!
Thirty-eight years have swept by
At a mere snap of fingers.
And now we can go
Up the ninth heaven to pluck the moon,
Down in all five seas to catch turtles.
Talking and laughing,
We'll return with songs of triumph.
Nothing is impossible in the world:
The knack is to keep surmounting.

A *tsu,* to the melody *Water's Music: the Prelude, Shui-tiao Ko-tou.*

Written in May 1965 when Mao was re-visiting the Mountain on an inspection trip — 38 years after he established there the first rural base of Red power. The poem is a song of the Chinese people's victory in those stirring years of revolution and reconstruction, but still more, a clarion call to fight on as the concluding lines indicate.

Huangyangkai: the most imposing of the five strategic passes leading up to Chingkang Mountain, where four successive attacks by Kuomintang troops were repulsed in August 1928 (see Poem III and notes).

Moon-plucking, presumably alluding to the high aspirations and endeavors of building up new China, is derived from lines by the Tang poet Li Po:
    Full of wild fancies, we let soar our daring thoughts,
    Ready to pluck the moon in a flight up the blue sky.

Turtle-catching: "Catching a turtle in an urn" is an ancient saying, meaning an adversary cornered and easily caught. The epithet as used in the poem alludes ironically no doubt to the forces of reaction the world over, particularly Soviet revisionism.

XXXIX
Two Birds: A Dialogue

Autumn 1965

The whale-roc,
Wings spreading,
Strikes and soars
Ninety thousand *li* up
Over the goat's horn of the hurricane.
Back against the blue,
He casts a look downward:
The world of men,
Walls and towns —
Shells pitting the earth,
Gunfire raging in space.
The sparrow in his bush
Drops prostrate and dazed.
"This is the doom, alas me!
I'll have to flit and flee."

"Whereto, sir, I pray?"
"To the Isle of Immortals,"
The sparrow replies,
"With palaces of jade!
Don't you know
Two years ago
When bright was the autumn moon,
The three of us families
Did a pact conclude?
And things galore there to eat too —

Potatoes piping hot
With beef to boot!"
"Wind and baloney!
Look you, the universe is overturning."

A *tsu*, to the melody *Fair Nien-nu, Nien-nu Chiao.*

A satire written in autumn 1965, a year after the fall of Khrushchev followed by intensified Khrushchevism in Soviet Russia.

Whale-roc: A parable in *Chuangtsu* (3rd century B.C.) tells of a whale in the North Sea transforming into a giant roc, who in his preparation for a migration to the South Sea soared 90,000 *li* up in the sky over the "goat's horn" (i.e. the whirling curve) of the hurricane, and who was mocked for this titanic undertaking by a tiny sparrow smugly stalled in its bush. Mao is making full use of this ancient parable — with a difference of course. The whale-roc need not be taken to mean the poet himself; it may well represent in his mind true Marxists in general. The sparrow alludes to Khrushchev and his successors. The formal publication of the poem in 1976 signalizes presumably China's unflinching resolve to carry on the ideological combat with Soviet Russia and the concomitant fight against super-power hegemony.

Isle of Immortals, alluding to the utopia of peace and prosperity held out by the Khrushchevians, is derived from an ancient legend about "Three Isles of Immortals in the East Sea," where Emperor Wu of the Han dynasty vainly sought to procure the elixir of life.

Three families' pact refers to the Treaty on the Partial Halting of Nuclear Tests signed by the Soviet Union, the United States and Great Britain on August 5, 1963.

Potatoes and beef alludes to Khrushchev's "goulash communism," so-called because of a speech he made in Hungary April 1, 1964 where he likened communist society to "a good dish of goulash" accessible to. all.

The universe overturning alludes evidently to the current world-wide struggles for national liberation and people's revolution as part of the historic process toward what the poet calls elsewhere "the radical social change throughout the world" in the "earth-shaking era" of the next 50 to 100 years.

The free mélange of classical vocabulary with vernacular and even vulgar is a stroke of literary audacity that carries a step further the practice shown in Poem XXXVI.

The following 3 poems, newly published in Chinese newspapers, are translated and incorporated here as an addendum in the present version without re-setting the order of the previous 39 poems.

- Translator

XXXX
An Untitled Piece

1923

A hand waving
And I'll be off!
Hard it is
That we stand here
Facing each other sorrow laden,
And once again dip in heart outpourings.
Regret seems to lurk behind our glances
And brood over the tips of our eyebrows.
Hot tears, welling up,
Are checked in vain.
Know then that about the previous letter
There has been a misunderstanding!
Floods of events
May keep rolling by,
Dense as fog.
You and I at least
Know each other and understand.
Ay, humans ail
If heaven sees!

Morning frost lies thick
Along East Gate Road.
The waning moon, half way down the sky,
Casts a gleam on the pool ahead,
So pale and so chill.
Then the blast of the whistle

To the break of our hearts!
Henceforth I'm destined to the sky's edge,
A lone traveller. —
But no! Away with these chains of sorrow,
And strings of regret!
Let us be as the Kunlun
That lops off its precipice,
Or the typhoon sweeping the earth.
We shall pair our wings again
And soar with the clouds!

A *tsu*, to the melody *Good Wishes to the Bridegroom, Ho Hsin-lang.*

October 1921, the Hunan Provincial Branch of the Chinese Communist Party was established with headquarters at Changsha. Here in an inconspicuous house outside the Little-Wu Gate, the poet worked with his wife Yang Kai-hui for nearly a year and a half when he had to leave Changsha for activities elsewhere. This poem was written in early 1923 as he was parting with Yang. Yang, it may be noted, joined Mao later as an active participant in the revolutionary struggles in Shanghai, Canton, Wuhan and elsewhere until she met her death at the hands of the Hunan warlords in November 1930.

This poem should be read in conjunction with Poem XXVI to get a full view of the deep sentiment the poet held for Yang. The formal publication (September 1978) for the first time of this lyric of a pronouncedly personal intimate note is significant as an added signal to remove the taboo imposed by the "gang of four" on taking love as a theme in art and literature.

XXXXI

On the Death of Comrade Lo Jung-huan

December 1963

I often think of the hectic days
When we were "fleeting over the grass"
And how seldom we found occasions to meet
Though we both were in the Red Army.
But the Long March after all
Wasn't such an overmuch trial.
It was the Battle for Chinchow
That brought along the real test.
The sparrow in the bush, as you know,
Would forever jeer at the giant roc.
And didn't the fluffy hen too
Itch to hold the eagle up to ridicule?
To our grief and loss now,
You've departed from this world.
To whom should the nation turn for counsel
When faced with challenge and doubt?

A *shih* in seven-word regular, *Chi Lu.*

Lo Jung-huan: one of the "Ten Marshals" of New China. He took part in the Autumn Harvest Uprising led by Mao Tse-tung in 1927, went up to Chingkang Mountain with Mao soon afterwards and remained a faithful follower of Mao's military line until his death in winter 1963.

The conversational tone in which this poem is written suggests a personal intimacy and a tête-à-tête communion of thoughts as found in Poem XXII with the same effect.

Fleeting over the grass, a literary expression for fast travel with light provisions, alludes here to the swift movement and tense life of the Long March days. Lo was then a leading cadre in the political section of the First Force of the Red Army. He went with the vanguard and often had to cover a hundred *li* a day in face of constant enemy attacks. "In spite of his ill health," commented Mao once, "Lo weathered the storm of the Long March days. He not only had to fight perpetually with the enemy but also took an unflinching stand in the fierce struggles within the Party." Mao here was referring, no doubt, to the opportunist oppositions of Wang Ming and Chang Kuo-tao. (See notes under Poems VIII, IX, XII and XVII.)

Battle for Chinchow, October 9-15, 1948, marked the decisive turning point in the Liaoning-Shenyang Campaign. For with capture of Chinchow, the Red Army was able to drive south against the demoralized forces of the Kuomintang, culminating in the annihilation of 470,000 enemy men on November 2 and the consequent liberation of the whole of northeast China. As political commissar of the Northeast Force, Lo was the chief upholder of Mao's strategy for the campaign as against Lin Piao's attempt to switch the drive northward to Changchun.

Sparrow and roc: See note under Poem XXXIX.

Hen and eagle: derived from I. A. Krylov's fable, where an eagle once happened to alight on the top of a hayloft and was ridiculed by a hen for having no more ability to fly higher than any common fowl.

On history

Spring 1964

With a hasty salute
Man parted with the ape.
Sundry polished stones
He made in his infancy.
Bronze and iron were then
Turned and tossed in flaming furnaces.
How long since, you ask?
A few thousand shifts, I figure,
Of summer and winter, or thereabouts.
Occasions for smiles and laughter
Were rare in this world of men.
Battles flared and raged —
Bows bent at one another,
Terrains washed in blood.

This chronicle reviewed,
Snow whirls overhead,
Leaving behind but a dim memory
Of bits of scattered traces of a sterile past.
The holy deeds paraded
Of the Five Emperors and Three Sovereigns
Were only hoaxes played upon
The endless troops of passers-by.
Any real heroes and saints?
Yes, the glory that was Chih the Outlaw
And Chuang the Free-booter,

Followed by the mighty rise of King Chen
Wielding his golden axe!
The song is not all sung
When day breaks in the east.

A *tsu,* to the melody *Good Wishes to the Bridegroom, Ho Hsin-lang.*

Man's career is here depicted in a few graphic strokes, beginning with his differentiation from the ape down through the stone, bronze and iron ages — with, however, a sharp comment on the barrenness and falsity of the past and a spirited re-assessment of the revolts of the slaves and peasants, culminating in the advent of the proletarian revolution symbolized by the coming of the dawn.

Five Emperors and Three Sovereigns: legendary kings in ancient China, used here to represent ruling classes in general.

Chih the Outlaw and *Chuang the Free-booter:* Tao Chih（盗 跖）and Chuang Chueh（莊 蹻）, leaders of slave revolts in the 5th and 4th centuries B.C. respectively.

King Chen: Chen She（陈 涉）, the first peasant leader to raise the standard of revolt against the tyrannous Chin rule in 209 B.C.

[End]

Appendix

Chinese Originals of the Poems

I At Changsha

沁园春
长　　沙
一九二五年

独立寒秋，
湘江北去，
橘子洲头。
看万山红遍，
层林尽染；
漫江碧透，
百舸争流。
鹰击长空，
鱼翔浅底，
万类霜天竞自由。
怅寥廓，
问苍茫大地，
谁主沉浮？

携来百侣曾游。
忆往昔峥嵘岁月稠。
恰同学少年，
风华正茂；
书生意气，
挥斥方遒。

指点江山，
激扬文字，
粪土当年万户侯。
曾记否，
到中流击水，
浪遏飞舟？

II Golden Crane Tower

菩 萨 蛮

黄 鹤 楼

一九二七年春

茫茫九派流中国，
沉沉一线穿南北。
烟雨莽苍苍，
龟蛇锁大江。

黄鹤知何去？
剩有游人处。
把酒酹滔滔，
心潮逐浪高！

III Chingkang Mountain

西 江 月

井 冈 山

一九二八年秋

山下旌旗在望，

山头鼓角相闻。
敌军围困万千重，
我自岿然不动。

早已森严壁垒，
更加众志成城。
黄洋界上炮声隆，
报道敌军宵遁。

IV War between Chiang and Kwangsi Warlords

清 平 乐

蒋桂战争

一九二九年秋

风云突变，
军阀重开战。
洒向人间都是怨，
一枕黄粱再现。

红旗跃过汀江，
直下龙岩上杭。
收拾金瓯一片，
分田分地真忙。

V   Double-Nine Festival

采 桑 子

重　　阳

一九二九年十月

人生易老天难老，
岁岁重阳。
今又重阳，
战地黄花分外香。

一年一度秋风劲，
不似春光。
胜似春光，
寥廓江天万里霜。

VI   New Year's Day

如 梦 令

元　　旦

一九三〇年一月

宁化、清流、归化，
路隘林深苔滑。
今日向何方，
直指武夷山下。
山下山下，
风展红旗如画。

VII On the Road to Kwangchang

减字木兰花

广昌路上

一九三〇年二月

漫天皆白，
雪里行军情更迫。
头上高山，
风卷红旗过大关。

此行何去？
赣江风雪迷漫处。
命令昨颁，
十万工农下吉安。

VIII From Tingchow to Changsha

蝶 恋 花

从汀州向长沙

一九三〇年七月

六月天兵征腐恶，
万丈长缨要把鲲鹏缚。
赣水那边红一角，
偏师借重黄公略。

百万工农齐踊跃，
席卷江西直捣湘和鄂。
国际悲歌歌一曲，
狂飙为我从天落。

IX Breaking through the First "Encirclement"

渔 家 傲
反第一次大 " 围剿 "
一九三一年春

万木霜天红烂漫，
天兵怒气冲霄汉。
雾满龙冈千嶂暗，
齐声唤，
前头捉了张辉瓒。

二十万军重入赣，
风烟滚滚来天半。
唤起工农千百万，
同心干，
不周山下红旗乱。

X Breaking through the Second "Encirclement"

渔 家 傲
反第二次大 " 围剿 "
一九三一年夏

白云山头云欲立，
白云山下呼声急，
枯木朽株齐努力。
枪林逼，
飞将军自重霄入。

七百里驱十五日，
赣水苍茫闽山碧，
横扫千军如卷席。
有人泣，
为营步步嗟何及！

XI Tapoti

　菩 萨 蛮
大 柏 地
　一九三三年夏

　赤橙黄绿青蓝紫，
　谁持彩练当空舞？
　雨后复斜阳，
　关山阵阵苍。

　当年鏖战急，
　弹洞前村壁。
　装点此关山，
　今朝更好看。

XII At Huichang

　清 平 乐
会 昌
　一九三四年夏

　东方欲晓，

莫道君行早。
踏遍青山人未老，
风景这边独好。

会昌城外高峰，
颠连直接东溟。
战士指看南粤，
更加郁郁葱葱。

XIII Loushan Pass

忆 秦 娥

娄 山 关

一九三五年二月

西风烈，
长空雁叫霜晨月。
霜晨月，
马蹄声碎，
喇叭声咽。

雄关漫道真如铁，
而今迈步从头越。
从头越，
苍山如海，
残阳如血。

十六字令三首

一九三四年到一九三五年

山，
快马加鞭未下鞍。
惊回首，
离天三尺三。

其　　二

山，
倒海翻江卷巨澜。
奔腾急，
万马战犹酣。

其　　三

山，
刺破青天锷未残。
天欲堕，
赖以拄其间。

XVII The Long March

七　　律

长　　征

一九三五年十月

红军不怕远征难，
万水千山只等闲。

五岭逶迤腾细浪，
乌蒙磅礴走泥丸。
金沙水拍云崖暖，
大渡桥横铁索寒。
更喜岷山千里雪，
三军过后尽开颜。

XVIII Kunlun

念 奴 娇

昆　仑

一九三五年十月

横空出世，
莽昆仑，
阅尽人间春色。
飞起玉龙三百万，
搅得周天寒彻。
夏日消溶，
江河横溢，
人或为鱼鳖。
千秋功罪，
谁人曾与评说？
而今我谓昆仑：
不要这高，
不要这多雪。
安得倚天抽宝剑，
把汝裁为三截？
一截遗欧，
一截赠美，

一截还东国。
太平世界，
环球同此凉热。

XIX   Mount Liupan

清 平 乐
六 盘 山
一九三五年十月

天高云淡，
望断南飞雁。
不到长城非好汉，
屈指行程二万。

六盘山上高峰，
红旗漫卷西风。
今日长缨在手，
何时缚住苍龙？

XX   Snow

沁 园 春
雪
一九三六年二月

北国风光，
千里冰封，
万里雪飘。
望长城内外，

惟馀莽莽；
大河上下，
顿失滔滔。
山舞银蛇，
原驰蜡象，
欲与天公试比高。
须晴日，
看红装素裹，
分外妖娆。

江山如此多娇，
引无数英雄竞折腰。
惜秦皇汉武，
略输文采；
唐宗宋祖，
稍逊风骚。
一代天骄，
成吉思汗，
只识弯弓射大雕。
俱往矣，
数风流人物，
还看今朝。

XXI Occupation of Nanking by
the People's Liberation Army

七　　律
人民解放军占领南京
一九四九年四月

钟山风雨起苍黄，
百万雄师过大江。
虎踞龙盘今胜昔，
天翻地覆慨而慷。
宜将剩勇追穷寇，
不可沽名学霸王。
天若有情天亦老，
人间正道是沧桑。

XXII Reply to Mr. Liu Ya-tsu

七 律
和柳亚子先生
一九四九年四月二十九日

饮茶粤海未能忘，
索句渝州叶正黄。
三十一年还旧国，
落花时节读华章。
牢骚太盛防肠断，
风物长宜放眼量。
莫道昆明池水浅，
观鱼胜过富春江。

XXIII Reply to Mr. Liu Ya-tsu

浣 溪 沙
和柳亚子先生
一九五〇年十月

一九五〇年国庆观剧，柳亚子先生
即席赋浣溪沙，因步其韵奉和。

长夜难明赤县天，
百年魔怪舞翩跹，
人民五亿不团圆。

一唱雄鸡天下白，
万方乐奏有于阗，
诗人兴会更无前。

XXIV   At Peitaiho

浪 淘 沙
北 戴 河
一九五四年夏

大雨落幽燕，
白浪滔天，
秦皇岛外打鱼船。
一片汪洋都不见，
知向谁边？

往事越千年，
魏武挥鞭，
东临碣石有遗篇。
萧瑟秋风今又是，
换了人间。

水调歌头

游　　泳

一九五六年六月

才饮长沙水，
又食武昌鱼。
万里长江横渡，
极目楚天舒。
不管风吹浪打，
胜似闲庭信步，
今日得宽馀。
子在川上曰：
逝者如斯夫！

风樯动，
龟蛇静，
起宏图。
一桥飞架南北，
天堑变通途。
更立西江石壁，
截断巫山云雨，
高峡出平湖。
神女应无恙，
当惊世界殊。

XXVI Reply to Li Shu-yi

蝶 恋 花

答李淑一

一九五七年五月十一日

我失骄杨君失柳，
杨柳轻飏直上重霄九。
问讯吴刚何所有，
吴刚捧出桂花酒。

寂寞嫦娥舒广袖，
万里长空且为忠魂舞。
忽报人间曾伏虎，
泪飞顿作倾盆雨。

XXVII XXVIII Good-bye, God of Plague

七律二首

送 瘟 神

一九五八年七月一日

读六月三十日人民日报，余江县消灭
了血吸虫。浮想联翩，夜不能寐。微风拂
煦，旭日临窗。遥望南天，欣然命笔。

绿水青山枉自多，
华佗无奈小虫何！
千村薜荔人遗矢，
万户萧疏鬼唱歌。
坐地日行八万里，

巡天遥看一千河。
牛郎欲问瘟神事，
一样悲欢逐逝波。

其　　二

春风杨柳万千条，
六亿神州尽舜尧。
红雨随心翻作浪，
青山着意化为桥。
天连五岭银锄落，
地动三河铁臂摇。
借问瘟君欲何往，
纸船明烛照天烧。

XXIX　At Shaoshan

七　　律

到　韶　山

一九五九年六月

一九五九年六月二十五日到韶山。
离别这个地方已有三十二周年了。

别梦依稀咒逝川，
故园三十二年前。
红旗卷起农奴戟，
黑手高悬霸主鞭。
为有牺牲多壮志，
敢教日月换新天。
喜看稻菽千重浪，

遍地英雄下夕烟。

XXX   Ascending Lushan

七　　律
登 庐 山
一九五九年七月一日

一山飞峙大江边，
跃上葱茏四百旋。
冷眼向洋看世界，
热风吹雨洒江天。
云横九派浮黄鹤，
浪下三吴起白烟。
陶令不知何处去，
桃花源里可耕田？

XXXI   Militia Women:

　　　Inscription on a Photograph

七　　绝
为女民兵题照
一九六一年二月

飒爽英姿五尺枪，
曙光初照演兵场。
中华儿女多奇志，
不爱红装爱武装。

XXXII Reply to a Friend

七　律

答友人

一九六一年

九嶷山上白云飞，
帝子乘风下翠微。
斑竹一枝千滴泪，
红霞万朵百重衣。
洞庭波涌连天雪，
长岛人歌动地诗。
我欲因之梦寥廓，
芙蓉国里尽朝晖。

XXXIII Fairy Cave, Lushan: Inscription on a Photograph

七　绝

为李进同志题所摄庐山仙人洞照

一九六一年九月九日

暮色苍茫看劲松，
乱云飞渡仍从容。
天生一个仙人洞，
无限风光在险峰。

XXXIV Reply to Comrade Kuo Mo-jo

七　律

和郭沫若同志

一九六一年十一月十七日

一从大地起风雷，
便有精生白骨堆。
僧是愚氓犹可训，
妖为鬼蜮必成灾。
金猴奋起千钧棒，
玉宇澄清万里埃。
今日欢呼孙大圣，
只缘妖雾又重来。

XXXV The Winter Plum

卜　算　子

咏　　梅

一九六一年十二月

读陆游咏梅词，反其意而用之。

风雨送春归，
飞雪迎春到。
已是悬崖百丈冰，
犹有花枝俏。

俏也不争春，
只把春来报。
待到山花烂漫时，
她在丛中笑。

XXXVI Winter Clouds

七　律

冬　云

一九六二年十二月二十六日

雪压冬云白絮飞，
万花纷谢一时稀。
高天滚滚寒流急，
大地微微暖气吹。
独有英雄驱虎豹，
更无豪杰怕熊罴。
梅花欢喜漫天雪，
冻死苍蝇未足奇。

XXXVII Reply to Comrade Kuo Mo-jo

满　江　红

和郭沫若同志

一九六三年一月九日

小小寰球，
有几个苍蝇碰壁。
嗡嗡叫，
几声凄厉，
几声抽泣。
蚂蚁缘槐夸大国，
蚍蜉撼树谈何易。
正西风落叶下长安，
飞鸣镝。

多少事，
从来急；
天地转，
光阴迫。
一万年太久，
只争朝夕。
四海翻腾云水怒，
五洲震荡风雷激。
要扫除一切害人虫，
全无敌。

XXXVIII　Chingkang Mountain Re-ascended

水 调 歌 头

重上井冈山

一九六五年五月

久有凌云志，
重上井冈山，
千里来寻故地，
旧貌变新颜。
到处莺歌燕舞，
更有潺潺流水，
高路入云端。
过了黄洋界，
险处不须看。

风雷动，
旌旗奋，
是人寰。

三十八年过去，
弹指一挥间。
可上九天揽月，
可下五洋捉鳖，
谈笑凯歌还。
世上无难事，
只要肯登攀。

XXXIX   Two Birds: A Dialogue

念 奴 娇

鸟儿问答

一九六五年秋

鲲鹏展翅，
九万里，
翻动扶摇羊角。
背负青天朝下看，
都是人间城郭。
炮火连天，
弹痕遍地，
吓倒蓬间雀。
怎么得了，
哎呀我要飞跃。

借问君去何方？
雀儿答道：
有仙山琼阁。
不见前年秋月朗，
订了三家条约。

还有吃的，
土豆烧熟了，
再加牛肉。
不须放屁，
试看天地翻覆。

XXXX   An Untitled Piece

贺 新 郎

一九二三年

挥手从兹去。
更那堪凄然相向，
苦情重诉。
眼角眉梢都似恨，
热泪欲零还住。
知误会前翻书语。
过眼滔滔云共雾，
算人间知己吾和汝。
人有病，
天知否？

今朝霜重东门路。
照横塘半天残月，
凄清如许。
汽笛一声肠已断，
从此天涯孤旅。
凭割断愁丝恨缕。
要似昆仑崩绝壁，
又恰象飚风扫环宇。

重比翼,
和云翥。

七　　律

吊罗荣桓同志

一九六三年十二月

记得当年草上飞,
红军队里每相违。
长征不是难堪日,
战锦方为大问题。
斥鷃每闻欺大鸟,
昆鸡长笑老鹰非。
君今不幸离人世,
国有疑难可问谁?

贺　新　郎

读　　史

一九六四年春

人猿相揖别。
只几个石头磨过,
小儿时节。
铜铁炉中翻火焰,
为问何时猜得?
不过几千寒热。

117

人世难逢开口笑，
上疆场彼此弯弓月。
流遍了，
郊原血。

一篇读罢头飞雪，
但记得斑斑点点，
几行陈迹。
五帝三皇神圣事，
骗了无涯过客。
有多少风流人物？
盗跖庄蹻流誉后，
更陈王奋起挥黄钺。
歌未竟，
东方白。

List of Names

English	*Pinyin*	Chinese
Chang Hui-tsan	Zhang Huizan	张辉瓒
Chang Kuo-tao	Zhang Guotao	张国焘
Chen She	Chen She	陈 涉
Chen Yi	Chen Yi	陈 毅
Chih	Zhi	(盗)跖
Chiang Kai-shek	Jiang Jieshi	蒋介石
Chia Tao	Jia Dao	贾 岛
Chia Yi	Jia Yi	贾 谊
Chou En-lai	Zhou Enlai	周恩来
Chou Shih-chao	Zhou Shizhao	周士钊
Chou Tien	Zhou Dian	周 颠
Chuang Chueh	Zhuang Jue	莊 蹻
Chung Chun	Zhong Jun	终 军
Chu Teh	Zhu De	朱 德
Chu Yuan	Qu Yuan	屈 原
Emperor Kwang-wu	Guangwu Di	光武帝
Genghis Khan	Chengjisi Han	成吉思汗
Han Yu	Han Yu	韩 愈
Ho Ying-chin	He Yingqin	何应钦
Hsiang Yu	Xiang Yu	项 羽
Huang Kung-lueh	Huang Gonglüe	黄公略
Hua To	Hua Tuo	华 佗
Kuo Mo-jo	Guo Moruo	郭沫若
Kuo Po	Guo Pu	郭 璞
Li Kung-tso	Li Kongzuo	李公佐
Li Li-san	Li Lisan	李立三
Lin Piao	Lin Biao	林 彪
Li Po	Li Bai	李 白
Li Shu-yi	Li Shuyi	李淑一
Liu Chih-hsun	Liu Zhixun	柳直荀
Liu Pang	Liu Bang	刘 邦
Liu Ya-tsu	Liu Yazi	柳亚子
Lo Jung-huan	Luo Ronghuan	罗荣桓
Lu Yu	Lu You	陆 游

English	*Pinyin*	Chinese
Mao Tse-tung	Mao Zedong	毛泽东
Shun	Shun	舜
Sung Yu	Song Yu	宋 玉
Sun Hao	Sun Hao	孙 皓
Sun Yat-sen	Sun Yixian	孙逸仙
Tan Yung-chih	Tan Yongzhi	谭用之
Tao Yuan-ming	Tao Yuanming	陶渊明
Tsao Tsao	Cao Cao	曹 操
Tsui Hao	Cui Hao	崔 颢
Wang Ming	Wang Ming	王 明
Yang Kai-hui	Yang Kaihui	杨开慧
Yao	Yao	尧
Yen Kwang	Yan Guang	严 光
Yu	Yu	禹

List of Geographical Names

English	*Pinyin*	Chinese
Canton	Guangzhou	广 州
Chang-an	Chang'an	长 安
Changchow	Changzhou	常 州
Changchun	Changchun	长 春
Changsha	Changsha	长 沙
Changting	Changting	长 汀
Chekiang	Zhejiang	浙 江
Chi-an	Ji'an	吉 安
Chiangyin	Jiangyin	江 阴
Chiehshih	Jieshi	碣 石
Chienning	Jianning	建 宁
Chienyeh	Jianye	建 业
Chinchow	Jinzhou	锦 州
Chinghai	Qinghai	青 海
Chingkang Mountain	Jinggang Shan	井冈山
Chingliu	Qingliu	清 流
Chinhuang Tao	Qinhuangdao	秦皇岛
Chinsha River	Jinsha Jiang	金沙江
Chungking	Chongqing	重 庆
Fuchun River	Fuchun Jiang	富春江
Fukien	Fujian	福 建
Hangchow	Hangzhou	杭 州
Hankow	Hankou	汉 口
Hanyang	Hanyang	汉 阳
Hopei	Hebei	河 北
Hsianghsiang	Xiangxiang	湘 乡
Hsiang River	Xiang Jiang	湘 江
Huaijen Tang	Huairen Tang	怀仁堂
Huangyangkai	Huangyangjie	黄洋界
Huchow	Huzhou	湖 州
Huichang	Huichang	会 昌
Hunan	Hunan	湖 南
Hunghu (Lake)	Honghu	洪 湖

English	Pinyin	Chinese
Hupei	Hubei	湖 北
Juichin	Ruijin	瑞 金
Kansu	Gansu	甘 肃
Kiangsi	Jiangxi	江 西
Kiukiang	Jiujiang	九 江
Kuling	Guling	牯 岭
Kutien	Gutian	古 田
Kwangchang	Guangchang	广 昌
Kwangsi	Guangxi	广 西
Kwangtung	Guangdong	广 东
Kweichow	Guizhou	贵 州
Kweihua	Guihua	归 化
Lake Kunming	Kunming Hu	昆明湖
Lake Poyang	Poyang Hu	鄱阳湖
Lanshan Peak	Lanshan Ling	岚山岭
Lantienpang	Lantianbang	兰田畈
Liaoning	Liaoning	辽 宁
Liping	Liping	黎 平
Loushan Pass	Loushan Guan	娄山关
Luchow	Luzhou	泸 州
Lungkang	Longgang	龙 岗
Lungyen	Longyan	龙 岩
Lushan	Lu Shan	庐 山
Luting	Luding	泸 定
Maoerkai	Maorgai	毛儿盖
Minshan	Min Shan	岷 山
Mountain Kunlun	Kunlun Shan	昆仑山
Mount Chungshan	Zhong Shan	钟 山
Mount Kuanyin	Guanyin Shan	观音山
Mount Liupan	Liupan Shan	六盘山
Nanchang	Nanchang	南 昌
Nanking	Nanjing	南 京
Ninghua	Ninghua	宁 化
Ningsia	Ningxia	宁 夏
Ningtu	Ningdu	宁 都
Paiyun Hill	Baiyun Shan	白云山

English	Pinyin	Chinese
Papaoshan	Babao Shan	八宝山
Peak Feifeng	Feifeng Shan	飞风山
Pearl River	Zhu Jiang	珠 江
Peipei	Beipei	北 碚
Peitaiho	Beidaihe	北戴河
Peking	Beijing	北 京
Pengtse	Pengze	彭 泽
Pohai	Bohai	渤 海
Puchou Mountain	Buzhou Shan	不周山
River Kan	Gan Jiang	赣 江
Shanghai	Shanghai	上 海
Shanghang	Shanghang	上 杭
Shansi	Shanxi	山 西
Shaoshan	Shaoshan	韶 山
Shensi	Shaanxi	陕 西
Shenyang	Shenyang	沈 阳
Sikang	Xikang	西 康
Sinkiang	Xinjiang	新 疆
Soochow	Suzhou	苏 州
Summer Palace	Yi He Yuan	颐和园
Szechuan	Sichuan	四 川
Taiwan	Taiwan	台 湾
Tapoti	Dabodi	大柏地
Tatu River	Dadu He	大渡河
Tibet	Xizang	西 藏
Tien An Men	Tian An Men	天安门
Tingchow	Tingzhou	汀 州
Ting River	Ting Jiang	汀 江
Tsangwu	Cangwu	苍 梧
Tsunyi	Zunyi	遵 义
Tungting Lake	Dongting Hu	洞庭湖
Tungwei	Tongwei	通 渭
Wayaopao	Wayaobao	瓦窑堡
Wuchang	Wuchang	武 昌
Wuhan	Wuhan	武 汉
Wu Ling	Wu Ling	五 岭
Wumeng	Wumeng	乌 蒙

English	Pinyin	Chinese
Wushan	Wu Shan	巫　山
Wuyi Mountain	Wuyi Shan	武夷山
Yangtse	Chang Jiang	长　江
Yellow River	Huang He	黄　河
Yenan	Yan'an	延　安
Yipin	Yibin	宜　宾
Yuchiang	Yujiang	余　江
Yunnan	Yunnan	云　南
Yutu	Yudu	于　都

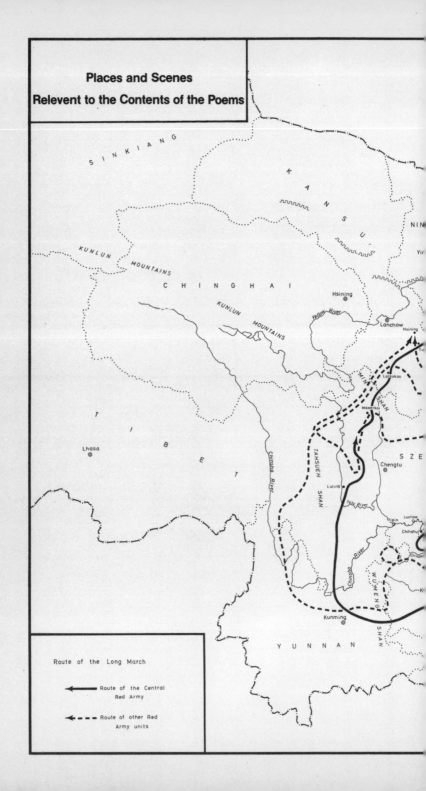

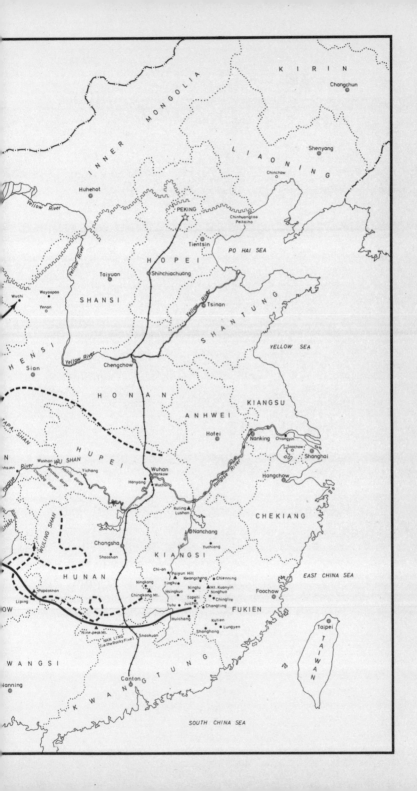